CAPITALMOMS

*A Firm Foundation for
All Seasons of Mompreneurship*

A Practical, Legal, and Spiritual Resource

Ebony Todd, Esq. and Shinia Lambert, Esq.

Renown Publishing
www.renownpublishing.com

CapitalMoms / Ebony Todd and Shinia Lambert
ISBN-13: 978-1-952602-94-8

To our mothers, our original CapitalMoms.

CONTENTS

CapitalMoms on a Mission

Thank you.

Thank you for reading this book. Thank you for investing in yourself and your business. Thank you for trusting us to pour into you what we believe God has given us to pour.

When the two of us met a few years ago, we had *zero* idea what was ahead. We were simply two attorneys in a courthouse being introduced by another attorney. We cordially acknowledged one another without the slightest idea that we were to become "life" (because we do more than business) partners in about a year.

We very quickly trusted one another enough to do business together and haven't looked back. Since then, we've felt a calling to help other mothers do business as well.

God knows, no mom should have to raise children alone, but so many of us do. In fact, there are more single mothers than married mothers in the U. S. workforce.[1] Whether you're single or married, we can all attest that raising children is something we should do *with* support.

The same goes for our businesses. We may be the only owner or have partners; either way, we should all seek support to "raise" our businesses. We've been blessed to support one another throughout this journey of being mompreneurs (moms *and* entrepreneurs)—or, as we like to say, "CapitalMoms." Entrepreneurs need financial capital to start, operate, and grow a business, but we believe that mutual support is also key. And now we're on a mission to support and encourage you, too!

You may be thinking, *"What exactly is a CapitalMom?"* She is a nurturer and a provider. She's about her God, her family, and her business. She's the big *M*, not the little *m*.

We were ultimately willed into writing this book after a single "CapitalMom" expressed concern to us about who would have custody of her children when she died and how her children would inherit the real property she had so diligently worked to acquire.

Maybe you've had those questions, or maybe you didn't know that you should have those questions. We've written this book to address many concerns, including some that you might never have known to have.

Throughout the book, we've included Bible verses and discussions of God and Jesus as a reflection of our faith and how the Lord has been a part of our life and business journeys. You'll also notice that the chapters are written in seasons and months, to be analogous with the seasons of business. In business, as in life, you may have winter, spring, summer, and autumn seasons. You will find three chapters, one for each month, that correlate with each season of business. They are intended to edify, empower, and educate you.

At the end of each chapter, you'll find a section entitled "It's Due Season!" These sections include challenges, exercises, and affirmations. By participating, you're taking control and ensuring that you will leave "in due season" with an eye toward *your* due season.

Now, we won't lie to you and say that the road has been easy. Indeed, in recent years, the two of us have endured business partnership changes, a pandemic, homeschooling, pregnancy, fluctuation in clientele and business, law practice changes, and defamation, not to mention a gamut of other personal concerns. But we can proudly say that we are unregretful.

We want the same for you. (Not the part about the issues!) We want you to do business without regret.

So please continue to read, and don't stop reading until the end. (Obviously, you can and should take breaks, but we think you know what we mean!) Like a course book or the Holy Bible, this resource should be read over time and consulted throughout different seasons. You may even want to reread. You may also want to schedule a consultation with an attorney or have a therapy session with your counselor or spiritual advisor—we won't judge. You'll get nothing but love and support from us.

Please keep in mind that this book is not intended to be legal advice, nor should it replace the legal, spiritual, or personal advice you can and should acquire from competent professionals. All content, materials, and information should be used for general informational purposes only. We want you to use this book as a guide, not as law or a rule. Don't act simply based on the information provided. Instead, may the information prompt you to ask more questions and convince you to gain more answers.

We want you to be spiritually, emotionally, and mentally sound as you embark on this wonderful journey of mompreneurship with us. Allow it to be a light read. We recommend that you don't get bogged down in legalese or other terms that may require additional research later. If that happens, consider making a note in the margins or adding a sticky note. Finish the chapter. Then return to your note and reread that portion once you have a fuller picture. If that doesn't help, discuss your questions with a competent professional.

As you work through this book, check in with your new community on Facebook in the CapitalMoms™ Group. Post your progress, questions, and wins!

You've got this! We know that you're not reading this for nothing—so here goes *something*.

—**Ebony and Shinia ("Shai")**

PART ONE: WINTER

December:
Making a List and
Checking It Twice
Ebony Todd

Establishing a firm foundation for success begins with a
plan.

—Author Unknown

Plan [noun]: a memorialized map of how you intend
to live out a vision or achieve a goal.

When I started my first business, I had no idea how to go
about actually starting it. I didn't even know what "it" was
until I attended an empowering women's event called God-
fidence Live, by Marshawn Evans Daniels. When Mrs.
Daniels encouraged us all to start with what we know, I knew
that I had to open a law firm. I had been trained in law school
and by the United States Army. I know law. So I did a great

deal of research specifically on my interest: law firms and business ownership. I also began to cultivate relationships in hopes of finding a mentor.

Though I did my homework, it would have been beneficial to have someone walk alongside me during my preparation period. Someone who had faith and useful experiences. Someone whom I could trust to want my success and not hinder my progress with her own agenda.

We want to be "someone" for you. That's why, in this book, we've compiled what we hope to be inspiration and guidance to help you build a solid foundation to start your business. We want you to start strong, right out of the gate, and we trust that the following information will help you to do just that!

WHAT'S YOUR VISION?

Most Christian women have heard about the "Proverbs 31 woman." This proverbial "virtuous and capable" woman (Proverbs 31:10 NLT) works very hard. For me, the exciting part of rereading Proverbs 31 was realizing that she, like you and I, has an entrepreneurial spirit. It's in the text that:

1. "She goes to inspect a field and buys it" (Proverbs 31:16 NLT).

2. "She makes sure her dealings are profitable" (Proverbs 31:18 NLT).

3. "She makes belted linen garments" (Proverbs 31:24 NLT).

As a mompreneur, the verse that most stands out to me is: "Her children stand and bless her. Her husband praises her" (Proverbs 31:28 NLT).

Wow. How amazing it must feel to be called blessed by your family. The family you work so hard for on a daily basis. The family you stay up into the wee hours of the morning for. The family whom you may often feel unappreciated by. Could it be that the thing that unites the vision of most mompreneurs is simply to be called blessed by those we love the most?

Although that's absolutely my vision now, I didn't grow up with it. When I was a little girl, I was sure that I'd be a doctor. In my early education planning, I took the medical track in high school to be better prepared for medical school. When I arrived on Baylor University's campus in 2004, I knew exactly what I was going to do with my life. I had everything planned to a T and under control.

Little did I know just how difficult biology classes would be at the old Baptist university. I had assumed that the professor would have a bit more grace and mercy on me. After all, being a doctor was my only life plan and vision!

At the end of my freshman year, I clearly needed to chart a new career path. That summer, I spent time in the Word (the Bible) and felt the Lord leading me to pursue the legal field. Now I'm not only an attorney, but also an appointed Associate Municipal Court Judge. I've served in the Army as an attorney as well and was paid to rappel from a helicopter! I didn't start with this vision, but when my son tells his teachers that his mom is an attorney, I can't help but feel that it's his way of calling me blessed.

Now, I'm not saying that deciding what to do with your life always comes as easily as reading Scripture. That said, I do believe that participating in the following activity can at least give you vision to head in the right direction. I call this activity "She R. A. N."

Reflect

Starting with your childhood and continuing up to the present, write a list of experiences that make you unique. What are your gifts and talents? What are you passionate or enthusiastic about?

While I was in high school, I was emotionally, mentally, spiritually, and scholastically preparing to become a doctor, yet there were certainly indications that law was another interest of mine. For instance, I served as an attorney for teen court in high school, and I loved it. Also, I was elected Governor of North Carolina's Girls State. My mom often said that I had a rebuttal for everything. Although it seemed insignificant at the time, she told me to "save it for the courtroom" more times than I'd care to admit. These experiences and others affirmed in my heart what God was telling me to do next in my life.

Assess

Completing a personality assessment is a great way to appreciate who you truly are to the core. Some common personality tests are the Myers-Briggs Type Indicator, the Caliper Profile, the Sixteen Personality Factor Questionnaire, and the SHL Occupational Personality Questionnaire, to name a few. Once you've completed an assessment, couple the results with your list of talents, gifts, and everything else that you're good at, including the mundane. Be sure to add to your list what other people believe that you do well.

For example, I am an encourager and a people person with a Type A personality. People recognize my ability to orate, author short stories and poetry, and recite information creatively. Though it may seem mundane, I also enjoy writing down my goals and tasks, and I have a particular fetish for achieving them. All of these gifts, talents, and tendencies help me with entrepreneurship and advocacy.

It may also be useful for you to write down the things that you don't enjoy or are not very good at. This will help you to make decisions about what you may need training in and what you should delegate. In my case, I don't enjoy budgeting, accounting, posting on social media, cooking, or cleaning (please don't judge me). I took that information and found a partner who is much better than I am at the business-related items on that list. I also order meal kits to be delivered to my door, and I sacrifice some of my spending habits to have housekeeping visit twice a month.

Network

Once you've identified *what* you'd like to do, make a point to speak with three other individuals in that field. With this exercise, it may help to start with individuals who are not in your geographical area to avoid future rivalry and unnecessary intimidation. I once offered to intern for free for a local attorney. He declined my offer because he was concerned that I would later become his competition. (Don't worry! It worked out because his *denial* was a part of God's systematic *direction* that made me the mompreneur I am today.)

In the event that you are planning to do something unique, try speaking with someone who is successful at doing something unique, even if it's in a different industry from yours. I'm also a fan of offering lunch and sending thank-you gifts or cards, as appropriate. Try writing a list of questions ahead of time and the answers that speak to your vision, as well as anything else you may be compelled to record.

If you complete these exercises, along with prayer and fasting, I don't doubt that you'll envision your "what" and hit the ground running. (We'll talk about prayer at points throughout this book, and in the September chapter, we'll take a more in-depth look at fasting.)

EVERY *WHAT* CAN BE ENTREPRENEURIAL

No matter what you decide to do, you can do it as an entrepreneur. My mother, Sabrina, was a military spouse. She was a hairstylist and enjoyed having her own business. As is normal in the military, we moved about every three years. With each move, my mother would rekindle her entrepreneurial vision and restart her business by finding the perfect location and then building her clientele—all before social media was a thing! She was determined, and she put in the hard work. She managed to operate multiple six-figure hair salons as a military spouse!

When I first left the Army, I planned to get a government job. I wanted something predictable and stable. However, I realized that it wouldn't provide the flexibility or earning potential I desired as a military spouse. With my mother's support and example, I was able to muster up the confidence and determination to start my own business.

Whether you're crafty, pack the tastiest and healthiest lunches, or homeschool well, every "what" can be entrepreneurial. Deciding to become an entrepreneur was not as intimidating with my mother around, but my prayer is that your confidence is boosted by this book and your decision to start your own business will be confirmed by the information and resources we share on these pages.

PREPARATION IS EVERYTHING!

Have you wondered why this book begins with December instead of January? Just as the seasons offer a cyclic rotation, conjoining the end of one year and beginning of the next, so do entrepreneurial seasons. By December, we have prepared and decided our goals for the New Year. Similarly, the journey of entrepreneurship should begin with planning and preparation.

A big part of your work at this stage is to make productive working lists and plans for how you can legally prepare yourself and your business before you start. In fact, list-keeping and planning are so essential that they should be maintained through the life cycle of your business. It may seem elementary, but I believe that lists and plans are a lost art in our world today. Some experts believe that handwriting is becoming a lost art and that this loss is negatively impacting automaticity (the ability to do a task, like driving, without thinking about it). There are so many benefits to writing, listing, and planning, an entire book could be written on those topics, but we'll focus on our businesses.

When beginning a business or starting a new business goal, written plans can be what gets you to take the allegorical leap. For instance, I'm constantly encouraging my friend, who is a single mother, to take the leap from teaching to real estate. She's a natural hustler and has a knack for all things real estate. I think that the only thing holding her back is a fear of leaving behind a steady paycheck. The risk is worth the reward from my point of view, but I realize that my friend is much more practical and reasonable than I am. I challenged her to do the following:

1. Write down how much you want to make each month, realistically and out of the gate.

2. Then write down how many homes you would need to sell and at what price point you would need to sell them in order to meet that goal.

3. Also write down any other creative way you could earn money to supplement your income. (For my friend, I recommended substitute teaching and notarizing documents, as she's a trained notary as well).

4. Review the plan at least biweekly to ensure that you remain conscientious of your goals and to determine if you should adjust your plans for the next two weeks.

I knew that seeing these figures on paper would allow her to see that her goals are not outrageous. Just the opposite: they are totally realistic and achievable. It's not just her dreamer of a friend, Ebony, making it up! She immediately thanked me for the challenge and told me that it was a game-changer for her. I believe that it can be a gamechanger for us all—whether we're hiring an employee, purchasing new equipment, leasing a building, or whatever else it may be. If the goal costs are significant and would require budget adjustments, this activity can truly make what appears to be a daunting objective much more achievable.

Let me make something very clear: I'm not telling you to quit your day job! In fact, it may be feasible and best for you to keep working while you start your business. It is 100 percent doable for you to start a business while still working for someone else (unless there is a policy or contract to the contrary). The point I'm making is that you should be strategic in your thinking and prepare to transition from working for someone else to working for yourself.

For mompreneurs, every day in business is a risk. That's exciting, but it can also be scary. (We'll address common fears in business in the October chapter.) Let's face it: living in the twenty-first century in our technology-driven world has left us easily distracted and constantly preoccupied, with short attention spans. When the world is spinning around us, the most basic way to enable dedication and goal achievement is taking the time to:

1. Write lists.

2. Create a business plan.

3. Memorialize your vision.

HOW TO WRITE TO-DO LISTS
THAT *WORK FOR YOU*

I'm sure that you've heard someone say, "Get it in writing!" As a practicing attorney, I know that writing everything down is vital. Why? Besides the legal advantages, written documents are a means of keeping people accountable.

To-do lists are a practical and important part of your preparation and planning when starting your business. When you write your lists, think of them as a contract with yourself, a form of accountability. The tasks I write on my daily lists are services I'm agreeing to provide and follow through on. Writing down daily goals can push your company forward further and faster. Dr. Gail Matthews of Dominican University in Stockton, California, conducted a study on goal setting and learned that a person is 33 percent more likely to accomplish a goal when it's written down, shared with a friend, and followed by weekly updates.[2]

Starting your business may seem even more daunting considering the plethora of other responsibilities you hold as a CapitalMom™. Something that has helped me personally to manage and accomplish tasks and goals that seem innumerable is to have them all listed together. I include my "home life" tasks on the same to-do list as my "work life" tasks. That way, I constantly review and remind myself to get them all done so that I don't forget about them—as often. I include tasks such as the following all on the same list:

- Taking my son to soccer practice
- Conducting legal research for a case
- Hiring a photographer for an event
- Attending a networking event
- Scheduling a hair appointment
- Drafting a client's contract

You may also strategically place tasks that you want to be sure to remember to do, no matter how mundane, at the top of the list—not because they're priorities, but so that you can read them each time you reference your list throughout your day. For me, listing soccer practice first reminds me to stop working early enough to get my son to practice. I'll have read soccer practice close to twenty times before the end of the day.

Sure, I could just set an alarm, but *seeing* the task throughout the day as I consult my list allows me to make a mental note of what lies ahead. When I do this, I can focus and prioritize critical tasks at hand before leaving work for the day to pick up my son. Not only am I able to prioritize tasks, but I also feel empowered to make adjustments to my schedule when necessary, which often isn't the case when a shrill (and often forgotten until the last minute) alarm is the only reminder I have to rely on.

I used to split home/personal and work/professional tasks across two lists, and I hardly ever got to my home/personal list! This made me feel terrible as a mother and a wife and negatively affected my confidence and mood.

As a side note, you may also wish to make lists with your children for their personal goals. You could make writing down tasks and goals a regular family activity. This promotes a healthy sense of goal setting and accomplishing, sets a brilliant example, and allows you to appreciate the goals of your children. Our family lists and reviews goals on Sundays and Wednesdays, respectively. (If you want to do a deep dive into the topic, I recommend *The One Minute Mother*, a book by Spencer Johnson, MD.)

WHAT ELSE SHOULD I INCLUDE ON MY LISTS?

New Business Lists

If you're just starting your business, you should have a list that includes things like:

1. Choose a business entity.

2. Research benefits and funding for my demographics and industry.

3. Obtain business capital.

4. File paperwork with the state to become a legal entity.

It isn't enough to list these tasks if you don't know where to begin. I also like to include questions and key reminders in my lists. Therefore, a more exhaustive list may look like:

1. Choose a business entity.

    a. Schedule a consultation with a business attorney.

    b. Research what business entities are in my state.

    c. Make a list of questions for the business attorney.

    d. Speak with a certified public accountant (CPA) and/or tax professional about business taxes.

2. Research benefits and funding for my demographics and industry.

    a. Google-search grants for my industry.

    b. Visit my local business resource center.

    c.   Find Facebook groups for my demographics and industry.

    d.   Join other organizations for my industry.

3.   Obtain business capital.

    a.   Determine how much money I need to get started.

    b.   Create a list of expenses.

    c.   Determine the cost of three months of expenses.

    d.   Budget to determine if I can manage the expenses myself or if I should obtain a loan or a grant.

    e.   Determine if I will need or want investors.

    f.   Determine what taxes I will have to pay.

4.   File paperwork with the state to become a legal entity.

    a.   Will I hire an attorney, or will I file myself?

    b.   If I'm going to do this on my own, what paperwork will I file, and how much will it cost?

    c.   If I'm going to hire an attorney, consult with attorneys to find a great fit and learn costs.

    d.   Obtain an Employer Identification Number (EIN) from the IRS. (This is also known as a

Federal Tax Identification Number, which is discussed more in the January chapter.)

  e. Obtain a state tax ID. (This is sometimes referred to as a state EIN.)

Business Goal Lists

The previous list structure can also be used for any new business goal. For example, if you're looking to hire a new employee, you may have a list that looks something like this:

1. Determine the proper job title for the employee.

   a. What responsibilities will help me to determine the title?

   b. What pay will suit the title?

2. Determine what I will pay the employee.

   a. What are the average pay rates for this job in this area?

   b. What can I do to ensure that the pay corresponds to the number and type of responsibilities?

3. Define the responsibilities of the position.

   a. What research can I do to find examples of responsibilities for this position in companies similar to mine?

    b.   What other duties should I add to this position?

4.   Pick the career websites to advertise the position.

    a.   Is this a job a student can handle?

    b.   Do I want several applicants or only a few?

    c.   Do I want someone I know or someone from outside my community?

5.   Identify who will interview and hire the employee.

    a.   Who needs this employee's assistance?

    b.   Who will benefit from the position?

6.   Draft interview questions.

    a.   What questions are illegal to ask?

    b.   What should I mention about our office culture?

    c.   What questions can I ask that illustrate what is important to our company?

7.   Determine how this will affect my taxes.

    a.   Should I contact the state's comptroller's office?

    b.   Should I contact the unemployment office?

8.   Determine whether the position may be filled by an independent contractor to save costs and liabilities.

What's important to note here is that you may not know what you don't know. That's okay! Sara Blakely, the founder of Spanx, says, "Don't be intimidated by what you don't know. That can be your greatest strength and ensure that you do things differently from everyone else." [3]

As an entrepreneur, you can tap into a vast number of resources to guide you on how to build your business's foundation. There is certainly no reason to enter the doors of entrepreneurship blindly. With all the free resources online, you could build your own empire if you're willing to put in the time to learn how.

WHAT NOW?

Once you have created your lists, the next thing to do is assign realistic due dates. Then add them to your phone calendar with alerts starting a week out.

Be practical with each task. Just as life is constantly changing, so should your goals and, therefore, your lists. I personally keep daily running lists on my desk and with me when I leave. That may not be realistic for everyone, but even if you have a weekly or monthly list, that's a great start. I wouldn't recommend going beyond a monthly list, because the more time passes between your creation of one list and the next, the less likely it will be made or reviewed.

Be prepared to amend your lists while diligently seeking to achieve each goal. You must remain flexible because the information you gain along the way will result in new steps that need to be taken. Don't forget to write a check mark next to a task that you have completed! Completing the tasks on your list will give you a feeling of affirmation.

Sometimes it isn't feasible or recommended to achieve a certain goal or to complete a specific task. In that case, cross it off your list and thank God that your steps are ordered. He has purposefully caused a goal or a step to be unobtainable. With this confident mindset, unaccomplished tasks feel less like *failures* and more like *"direct-tours"*—detours that are the result of divine direction.

Please don't take what I just said to mean giving up at the first sign of resistance. That would obviously be counterproductive and unbiblical. (Have you read Moses's story in Exodus, chapters 7 to 12?) What I mean is that everything we think of or write down may not come to fruition. I believe that God will reveal to you, through your fasting and prayer, when you need to fight to achieve a goal and when you should take a different route. (There will be more on fasting and prayer in the September chapter.)

GREAT ENTREPRENEURS START GREAT BUSINESSES WITH GREAT BUSINESS PLANS

Notice that this section is not titled "Great Entrepreneurs Start Great Businesses with a Great Amount of Money"! That's because it isn't so. Judy Faulkner started America's leading medical record software-providing company, Epic, out of her basement. Judy Love and her husband opened their first gas station with a $5,000 loan from family. Britni

Ricard failed to pay an electricity bill to get her company, COTA Skin, off the ground, and she became a self-made millionaire within two years. Maybe you've heard of the unemployed single mother J. K. Rowling, who went from welfare to becoming a billionaire after having her Harry Potter book idea rejected twelve times. Now, that's what I call a CapitalMom!

What's more important than having money is having a plan. In fact, one of the most important things you can do as an entrepreneur is to create a business plan. A business is 30 percent more likely to grow and will have up to 50 percent more business if it has a formal business plan.[4]

A business plan can assist you with obtaining capital and serve as a blueprint to follow and update throughout the life of your business. Your plan is a living document that memorializes your business's goals and details the strategies by which your business will achieve its goals. Many of the tasks in the lists that we have already discussed are components of a business plan.

Business plans in today's online world can be drafted quickly, especially if you use resources such as the Small Business Development Center or LivePlan®. Either way, you should not only give yourself a due date to create the plan, but also ensure that you have due dates for each section and topic, as well as the research necessary to complete the plan.

VISION BOARDS, VISION SESSIONS, AND BEING A VISIONARY LEADER

God instructed Habakkuk the prophet to "write the vision" that he was given from God so that it would be understood and preserved (Habakkuk 2:2 KJV). When we have a vision and feel led to a certain line of business or called to service, we don't have to be prophets to write down and memorialize it. In fact, not writing down our visions could be a form of burying our talents (see Jesus' story about this in Matthew 25:14–30), especially if it results in us never acting on a vision.

Writing a vision should be plain and simple. We should be able to articulate the vision even if we aren't sure how we will accomplish it.

In the last few years, there has been an overwhelming influx of vision-board parties. Some people cut out pictures from magazines and stick them to poster boards to represent the year ahead that they hope to have.

I can appreciate a good party and a vision board. However, at our law firm, we offer what we call "Vision Sessions" for our business owners. In these sessions, we use sticky notes in assorted colors and write different tasks on each. One color of sticky notes represents our office tasks, and the other represents our client's goals and tasks. On the poster board, we write "3 months," "6 months," "9 months," and "1 year." We spend up to two hours matching a task with an appropriate time frame. This activity allows us to understand our clients' visions while managing their expectations of what we will do to help them achieve their goals.

For example, we have a client with whom we recently conducted a Vision Session, and we were able to achieve 90 percent of what was on the board within six months. We had another client with huge dreams. The initial Vision Session included goals of purchasing vehicles for the business, purchasing land and buildings, having several employees, starting other businesses, and much more. We like to believe that we aren't dream-crushers, but it felt like it when we had Vision Calls (follow-up calls to track progress and amend the vision board as needed) for his business. We grew to realize during the Vision Calls that our client didn't have the resources or the time to accomplish his goals within the time restraints he put on himself. Although he had the vision, drive, and competency to accomplish the goals, he needed more time and capital.

The lesson here is to have realistic time frames and goals among the challenging ones so that, if nothing else, at least some goals are always accomplished to keep the fire burning!

If you choose to conduct your own Vision Session, consider using one color of sticky notes to represent tasks of third parties and another to represent personal tasks needed to accomplish your goals in the time frame of your choice. As with the goals lists, you may add sticky notes in yet another color to represent goals for your children in the different time frames, such as "sign James up for violin lessons" in the three-month category, "mommy and me swim lessons with Naomi" in the six-month category, and "sign Michael up for soccer" in the nine-month category.

Keep great notes of your ideas and decisions. Even without a partner, you may want to take "meeting minutes." These can simply be a list of decisions you've made. This record of your decisions holds you accountable to those decisions, serves as a journal of sorts, and can also be used to show a court that you were functioning as a company in the event that your company is ever involved in a lawsuit (see "Liability" below).

While you're figuring out your timeline, keep in mind the popular adage that "a goal without a deadline is just a dream."

LIABILITY: AS AN ENTREPRENEUR, YOU'RE MORE EXPOSED THAN YOU THINK

As business attorneys, Shai and I are routinely asked by business owners and entrepreneurs about liability, which is the concept of having legal responsibility for something. Personal liability means that an individual is personally responsible under the law. It may require an individual's assets to be subject to a claim to include (but not be limited to) his or her bank accounts, vehicles, and homes. Before starting your business, you should have at least a basic understanding of liability.

Most entrepreneurs desire to avoid personal liability at all costs. Those entrepreneurs typically create a business entity, such as a limited liability company or a corporation, to shield themselves from most legal responsibility. Although it is absolutely in the best interest of business owners and their families to avoid personal liability, there are times when it may be impossible to avoid it. Here are three examples of when a business owner may be personally liable for his or her business:

1. The business owner never actually creates a separate entity with the state; he or she is the sole proprietor. This is when an individual begins to offer services or products without creating a business entity with the appropriate state agency's office. When no business entity is formed, the individual conducting business has unlimited liability and, therefore, is legally responsible for the company's losses and liabilities. Creating a business entity should not be confused with filing an Assumed Name Certificate (Texas) or other DBA (Doing Business As) Certificate. DBAs are not business entities and do not shield against personal liability.

2. A business owner commits an intentional tort or other crime. Intentional torts, such as assault, defamation, and fraudulent misrepresentation, committed by business owners may create personal liability for the business owner as well as liability for the separate business entity. The same would apply to crimes such as selling illegal substances or directing an employee to commit a crime.

3. When a business owner guarantees the loans of the business. Normally, new business owners seeking business credit and/or loans must sign the contracts on behalf of the company but must also sign in their capacity as a guarantor. This

25

means that the lender may hold the business owner personally liable for the debt if the company doesn't pay the entire amount due.

We don't always advise our clients to create a business entity that protects them from liability, but it is the rule of thumb. See the next chapter (January) for more information about the different business structures and why you should consider officially forming a business. Liability will also be covered in more detail in the April chapter.

MANAGING RISKS AND PREVENTATIVE LAW

While shielding your assets from liability, you should also attempt to prevent litigation, illegal activity, and other legal issues. This is referred to as preventative law. Some entrepreneurs hire law offices on a retainer basis just to oversee legal issues as they come up. Other entrepreneurs use legal service providers such as LegalShield and LegalZoom. These legal platforms provide legal services at lower prices than most privately owned law firms. LegalShield offers prepaid legal plans while LegalZoom provides its services on an as-needed basis.

Our law firm, and some others, offer what we call "General Counsel Services." Our services assist clients with developing and executing systems that are intended to prevent unnecessary litigation, save money and time, and allow small businesses to operate like much larger firms.

Some preventative law measures all small-business owners should consider are:

1. *Business formation.* Although formation will be addressed more thoroughly in the January chapter, it's worth noting here that my earlier recommendation about taking "meeting minutes" is a great way of showing that your company is separate from you as an individual. It isn't enough for you to have a business. You need to operate as a business.

2. *Written contracts.* (See the March chapter.)

    a. Company agreements, operating agreements, or bylaws

    b. Non-compete clauses and agreements

    c. Non-disclosure agreements (NDAs) and confidentiality agreements

    d. Disclaimers

    e. Waivers

3. *Estate and business succession plans.* (See the September chapter.)

4. *Employee handbooks.* (See the February chapter.)

5. *Protecting intellectual property.* (See the April chapter.)

    a. Copyright

    b. Trademarks

    c. Patents

The Connection Between Faith and Success

After reading this chapter, you may be thinking, *"I don't know if I feel ready to do this."* Well, the answer to that is, you may never feel ready—most business owners don't. To succeed, you'll have to get started, anyway!

Do you need more inspiration? According to a Baylor University study, 34 percent of entrepreneurs pray several times a day, compared to 27 percent of non-entrepreneurs.[5] As Christian entrepreneurs, we are not alone on this journey. We have a greater power driving us. We have faith in the God who gave us the vision, and we must trust that God will bless our efforts, even if the results aren't always what we expect.

Be encouraged to *go*, sister! As I once heard a Christian speaker say, *"Go* is the first two letters of God's name!" You have a purpose to fulfill and a dream to live.

It's Due Season!

For this activity, have a blank piece of paper handy or write directly on the page.

As women made in God's image, we should reflect God in our plans, words, and actions. In the appropriate blanks below, write the name of your business (if you have one; if not, just write, "my business") and your goals. Then recite the following at least once every day for thirty days:

For I know the plans I have for _____
(the name of the business).

My goals are to (the goals of your business):

_____

_____

_____

_____.

My goals are for good and not for disaster, to give
_____ *(the name of your business) a*
future and a hope.

December Notes

January:
All Things New

Shinia Lambert

Behold, I am doing a new thing; now it springs forth, do you not perceive it? I will make a way in the wilderness and rivers in the desert.

—Isaiah 43:19 (ESV)

New [adjective]: not existing before; made, introduced, or discovered recently or now for the first time. Already existing but seen, experienced, or acquired recently or now for the first time.[6]

As a child, I loved the start of a new school year. It wasn't about the teacher, the classroom, or even the chance to make new friends. It was about one thing and one thing only: the school supplies. Oh, be still my heart! Picking out new color-coordinated school supplies, sectioning off my brand-new binders with bright tabs. There were pencils with holographic images and big, rubbery erasers in fun colors that I attached to the ends. Protractors! Rulers! Notebook paper (college, not wide ruled)! There's just something exhilarating about *new*.

THE PASSION OF A NEW START

Everyone needs a fresh start, and starting your own business is your chance! I love what motivational coach and author Barbara Sher said regarding the importance of learning something new. She stated, "You can learn new things at any time in your life if you're willing to be a beginner. If you learn to like being a beginner, the whole world opens up to you." [7]

No matter your age, your background, your ethnicity, and your educational level, you can learn how to start your business and be successful. The key to a fresh start comes down to passion. What motivates you?

We tend to be motivated in one of two ways, either intrinsically or externally. Intrinsic motivators, as the word implies, are those that are "inward." They are personal things that cannot be seen by the naked eye, such as what you believe, your hopes, your dreams, your passion, and your faith. These inward motivators keep you going in the face of challenges and setbacks because they are what fundamentally drives you in life.

External motivators can be just as engaging, but as the word implies, they are external rather than personal factors. Typical external motivators include awards, accolades, financial success, and promotions. Studies have shown that powerful, external motivation rarely lasts long term if an immediate award isn't given in exchange for certain types of behavior. That's why so many people don't keep their New Year resolutions and see them fade within the first quarter of the year.

THE "WHY" OF WHAT YOU ARE DOING

Your passion for a fresh start will have longevity when it's undergirded by purpose. In other words, what is the "why" of what you are doing? Though both external and intrinsic motivators are important, when it comes to starting a business and maintaining motivation, intrinsic motivators win out. I encourage you to be able to define clearly what yours are.

Start by asking yourself the questions below. Pray over them and ask God for wisdom in these areas. Don't be afraid to ask those closest to you who have integrity, are trustworthy, and can give wise counsel to help you see the qualities you possess and the blind spots of which you are not aware.

1. Who am I?

   a. How do I define myself?

   b. As a believer, do I understand my identity in Christ and the privilege and responsibility that accompany that identity?

    c. As an entrepreneur, do I know the unique gifts that I possess?

2. What am I called to do?

    a. Have I asked God how I should use what He has entrusted to me?

    b. What problem was I created to solve?

    c. What am I passionate about?

3. How do I define success?

    a. What is my source for defining success?

    b. What is important to me when I think about the reality of my life, family dynamics, and future goals?

4. What is at stake if I start my business this year?

    a. What financial decisions do I need to make?

    b. What emotional transactions am I ready to face?

    c. Is my family supportive?

    d. What sacrifices need to be made?

    e. Who will benefit?

    f. What needs will be met?

5. What is at stake if I don't start my business this year?

    a. What opportunities will I miss?

    b. Will I lose my confidence?

   c. Do I have peace about waiting?

   d. Have I heard clearly from God concerning His timeline?

I remember attending a virtual workshop on entrepreneurship at which the host discussed the need to have an exciting proposition. An exciting proposition is what you would tell people you were meeting for the first time when they ask you, "So, what do you do?"

The goal is to explain your mission succinctly and in a manner that makes the listener excited to hear more. Take time going over the questions listed above. They are designed to help you confidently identify and articulate what you've been called to do with that unique gift, talent, and passion that God has given you.

By thinking through these questions, seeking God's wisdom, and being willing to be honest with yourself, you can gain confidence in determining the right path to take. Don't feel a need to rush through these questions. The answers are the foundation for your "why." The "why" is what lies at the heart of your intrinsic motivation. It's what made you smile as a child and what keeps you up at night, imagining what could be. It's the reason you keep trying, even after a perceived failure.

FAITH AS YOUR MOTIVATOR

Your "why" boils down to your faith, what you sincerely believe to be true about God, yourself, and your life. You'll find motivation at the heart of your faith. My personal chief motivator is my desire to take God at His Word and experience the life I've been promised by the Creator of the universe.

God is my "why." That may seem too broad, but everything else I've used to fill my longing to be satisfied has always fallen short: struggles with perfectionism, fruitless relationships, and a never-ending pursuit of affirmation. However, when God remains my focus, I can walk into a place, season, or opportunity with confidence.

That same confidence can be yours. Knowing your "why" is critical. It puts things into the right perspective and helps you to work hard, make right choices and sacrifices, and juggle more than one task. Knowing your "why" means that when you make mistakes, when you're frustrated and exhausted, even when you're hurt, you still don't give up!

THE NEED FOR EXECUTING YOUR PLAN

Now that you've done the hard work of expanding your vision into manageable tasks, objectives, and lists, can we talk about execution? Did you know that only 2 percent of leaders believe that they can execute 80 to 100 percent of the plans they strategize?[8] How unfortunate that so much time is spent planning with so little faith that the plan will work out! It's an unsustainable way to lead a business.

Successful businesses not only create a great plan, but also know how to execute it. Execution is where your list making and goal setting are put into practice. It's where the rubber meets the road. It's the doing phase. It is, by the way, my favorite phase.

Now that you know what you're doing (as per all of your list making and goal setting in the December chapter) and why you're doing it (motivated by something deeply personal that exceeds temporary, external value and rewards), let's talk about how you execute.

There are four steps that will get you from where you are right now to where you dream of being, your promised land.

Step 1: Leaving Your Comfort Zone

In Deuteronomy 1, as God was leading His people out of Egypt and into their promised land, He told them to break camp and leave Mount Horeb. He was calling them to leave the place they had settled—the place that wasn't quite where they had started, but also wasn't the destination to which God was calling them. He was calling them out of their comfort zone.

Our comfort zone may look a little different from Mount Horeb, but as Mount Horeb did for the Israelites, it represents the place where we find ourselves dissatisfied, yet comfortable because of the familiarity. No matter how discontented we are with our lives, we are often more willing to accept another day, month, or year of the familiar, no matter how painful it is, than to risk a change.

T. D. Jakes once said in a sermon, "[You must] forsake your comfort to attain your destiny. And that's why most people will never evolve. Because they will not pay the cost of being uncomfortable. Excellence requires discomfort." [9]

I'm imploring you to leave the pit of your comfort zone as it relates to you and your business. You may not have to leave a physical place, but rather the mental place where you reside. One of the biggest challenges you will face when leaving your comfort zone is addressing the way you think about yourself, your business, and other people. In order to do that, you need to be willing to acknowledge those places, perspectives, and people that are holding you back.

Are you trying to revive things that need to die? Is that constant mental resurrection keeping you from believing who you are in Christ and what God says you can do? You must be willing to think new thoughts.

It's not enough to make the lists and to check them twice. It's time to start crossing things off the list! If your mindset is saturated with the belief that because it's hard, it's not meant for you, then you are believing a lie. Ease is no indication of calling. You need to be willing to let go of what no longer serves you to take hold of what satisfies you. Remember: all things new!

Step 2: You Must Be Willing to Endure the Testing That Will Prepare You for Your Purpose

When Moses led the people away from Mount Horeb, Scripture says that they traveled "through all that great and terrifying wilderness" (Deuteronomy 1:19 ESV). What did the wilderness signify? Times of trials and testing. There's really no way to pretty it up. This is a part of the process we need.

If it's what is standing between us and our success, then it's also what we want.

You can't take your comfort zone mentality into the promised land! What has been purposed for you to take hold of is far too great for you to lose due to lack of preparation. This wilderness, this in-between place where you may find yourself, holds the key to your transformation. You can and should expect your life to be shaken, shifted, and in some cases shattered—all for your own good.

I know that doesn't sound attractive at all. First, I tell you to leave your comfort zone, which will result in you're being uncomfortable. Now I'm saying that you need to be willing to be shaken up! You may be thinking, *"This is not what I signed up for."* But what if it's the only way to the other side? You are only passing through the wilderness on the way to your destination. It's only a segment of your path. Don't fear the process; it's all part of your journey!

Step 3: You Have to Be Brave and Continue to Believe Even When You Are in the Minority

As the Israelites approached the boundary line of their promised land, God told them to go in and conquer it! They sent in twelve men to scout out the unfamiliar territory (Numbers 13–14). Ten out of the twelve came back and shared a dreadful report. They said that Canaan was a land of great resources but was inhabited by powerful people in fortified cities. Some of these people were giants! However, two of the men, Caleb and Joshua, had a completely different perspective. They saw the same land, the same resources, the same obstacles, and they believed that God would give them the land as He had promised (Numbers 14:6–9). Caleb declared, "Let's go at once to take the land.... We can certainly conquer it!" (Numbers 13:30 NLT).

Now, before we judge the other ten men too harshly, whom do we more closely resemble when faced with obstacles? Do we still confidently believe God's promises and the direction He has already given us when we are faced with an unexpected challenge, a distracting delay, an unwarranted "no," or an unprecedented pandemic? Do we push forward when the work is demanding and there's no discernible end or reward in sight?

The desert place isn't arbitrary, and it's not meant to break you. It's designed to build you to the point of sure, steadfast, unshakeable faith and confidence!

Renee Swope famously said, "I want to be a woman who overcomes obstacles by tackling them in faith instead of tiptoeing around them in fear." [10] Having faith doesn't mean that the reality of your situation is pleasant or that you pretend not to see the very real challenges ahead. Having faith means that no matter what you see or don't see, feel or don't feel, experience or don't experience, you choose to believe God's promise. Even if what's in front of you seems to contradict what God has told you, you choose to believe His words.

This journey you're beginning is preparing you for the

moment when you stand on the boundary line of your promised land, your place of purpose and abundance, and are courageous enough to go in and possess it!

Step 4: Trust God's Will and His Timing

As believers, we have a calling on our lives to submit not only to God's "what," but also to His "when." When God commands us to move, we move. When God told the Israelites to go in and possess the land, they hesitated. When they later decided that they were ready to go in, God made it clear that He would not be with them. They went in anyway and were utterly defeated (Numbers 14).

You and I have the spiritual obligation to obey what our Father says when He says it, not when it seems right, sounds right, feels right, or looks right. When we do that, God indeed will bless us, our families, and our businesses!

TIME TO ROLL UP YOUR SLEEVES!

What if this year were different? What if you didn't just talk about going into business? What if you decide to lay aside all the excuses and instead make one intentional choice at a time to pursue your dreams and see your business excel? What if you really were to leave your comfort zone, endure testing, stay courageous, and trust God's timing?

World-renowned leadership expert John Maxwell has often said (and I'm paraphrasing here), "Tell me your goals, and I can tell you right now, based on what you've done today, if you'll ever reach them." It's the principle of sowing and reaping. You may have marvelous plans for your future. However, those plans will never come to fruition if you're not putting in the work.

Set the goal and plan to reap, but be mindful that you can reap only what you sow. Do you want to reap success? Work hard. Do you want to reap prosperous partnerships and relationships? Sow service and love for people.

It's time to roll up your sleeves and get to work! Your promised land is waiting.

STARTING OFF ON THE RIGHT FOOT: THE LEGAL FRAMEWORK OF SETTING UP YOUR BUSINESS

As attorneys who practice primarily business law, we applaud those who do their homework and research the various legalities involved in forming a business. We have also seen the many errors that people can make when they decide to forgo legal assistance in the formation of their businesses.

We in no way want to discourage you from setting up your business yourself. It certainly can be done. Most, if not all, states will provide resources and information to assist you on their respective Secretary of State websites. However, if you have the financial ability and the access to consult with a business attorney prior to forming your business, we highly recommend that you do so.

Recently, we had a client contact us because her relationship with her business partner had progressively declined. As a result, they agreed to review and revise their company agreement to realign responsibilities and reduce the partner's interest in the partnership. However, negotiations quickly deteriorated, and our client was considering parting ways with her business partner. The only problem was that they'd formed a partnership, and because they were the only two partners, if one left, there would be no partnership. In other words, they'd be out of business.

After reviewing her partnership agreement, we discovered that our client and her partner hadn't formed the business entity type they'd intended to form. In fact, they were operating and doing business as an improper entity that was improperly formed! And the company agreement? A disaster. Their formation documents were incorrect, with critical steps left incomplete, which put both our client and her business partner in a vulnerable position when it came to personal liability. The good news is that we were able to assist and help them reach a resolution that saved their business and their relationship. But unfortunately, that's not always the case.

These types of errors are common. It's far easier to get help from a business attorney and form your business the right way, at the onset, rather than get entangled later with the hassle and expense of litigation—or worse, losing your business altogether. At the very least, consider hiring a business attorney to conduct a document review to make sure that you're clear on *what* you're filing and *why*.

CHOOSING YOUR BUSINESS ENTITY TYPE

A business entity is a legal framework for your business, whether you are selling a product or a service. Each business type differs depending on the number of owners, personal liability, taxation, and how that business is going to be managed. The following is not intended to be an exhaustive list of every entity type and every factor you may want to consider. The goal is to give you a foundation and a place to start. I want to forewarn you that any talk regarding taxes is a personal snooze fest, but don't let that dissuade you from being educated. This is a spectacular opportunity to partner with a tax professional who can purposefully make the information palatable.

Two of the most well-known and popular business entities for small businesses, especially for mompreneurs (CapitalMoms!), are sole proprietorships and LLCs (Limited Liability Companies).

Sole Proprietorship (SP)

An SP is a business entity that has one owner who is doing business in his or her own name or operating with an assumed name (commonly referred to as a DBA, or Doing Business As), which is registered with the county clerk. This is the extent of any legal formalities. Be mindful if your state requires DBAs to be filed and under what circumstances. For example, in Texas, if you are doing business in any name other than your given name, you must file an Assumed Name

Certificate with the Secretary of State (SOS).

Liability: As an owner of an SP, you are personally liable for company debts, contractual performance, and any other business obligations, including those created by employees. This opens you up to more liability than you may feel comfortable with. If your business incurs a debt that it cannot pay, you're liable for it. If your employee gets into a car accident and is injured or the person your employee hit is injured, you'll pay for it. If a contractual obligation has gone unfulfilled for whatever reason, you're responsible. Everything you personally own can be part of a lawsuit.

So why would you want to be an SP? The answer is that it is the easiest business entity type to set up and the least expensive. In fact, if you're doing business right now and you've not registered with the Secretary of State, you're technically operating as an SP by default. Many who choose an SP view their business as something small that they intend to do on the side for now, and that's perfectly okay.

Taxation: SPs enjoy pass-through taxation to the owner. Taxes apply to a sole proprietor's income at individual rates. Gross income and deductions are reported on the individual's IRS 1040 Schedule C.

Management: The SP is, of course, managed by the sole owner.

Limited Liability Company (LLC)

An LLC is a flexible form of organization that many business owners find attractive. An LLC can be solely owned or have multiple owners. Owners (also referred to as "members") of LLCs own either all or a percentage of the company and either manage the company themselves or elect a manager.

An LLC is created by preparing and filing a formation document with the state. Names of all the owners must be disclosed in the certificate of formation, and all states require the original owners to sign the document. Amendments to the certificate of formation can easily be prepared and filed when there is a change of owners, managers, and/or management terms. There is typically also a company agreement or operating agreement.

Liability: There is no personal liability of the manager or owner for debts of the company. An LLC is an excellent choice for any business owner who would otherwise be personally liable for business obligations.

Taxation: An LLC is treated by default as a pass-through entity. If there is only one owner of the company, the LLC is treated as a "disregarded entity" for tax purposes with the Internal Revenue Service (IRS), and the owner reports the LLC's income or loss on Schedule C of his or her own individual tax return. An LLC with either a single member or multiple members may elect to be taxed as a corporation by filing IRS Form 8832. Some tax experts have recommended that an LLC be taxed as an 'S' Corporation for the best possible small business tax structure, combining the simplicity and flexibility of an LLC with the tax benefits of an 'S' Corporation.

Management: An operating or company agreement gives authority to a manager to manage the LLC, or the LLC can be managed by its owner(s).

General Partnership (GP)

A GP has an unlimited number of general partners. A partnership exists when two or more people form a business, with each having some form of management function. Without a written agreement between the partners, the IRS will presume that a partnership exists if profits from a business are shared. The proper title for a partnership is to identify it as a "Company." There is no legal requirement for a written partnership agreement.

Liability: Each general partner remains equally liable for all business debts and obligations to third parties. A GP doesn't differ much from an SP when it comes to personal liability, except the liability is spread over at least two people instead of the sole owner.

Taxation: The partnership must obtain a Federal Employer Identification Number (EIN) and register the assumed name of the entity in the county where it is located. A partnership files its annual tax return on IRS form 1065. Partnerships are pass-through entities, which means that the business entity itself pays no tax. The owners or partners are responsible for their individual share of taxes due from the business operations. Partners must report and pay taxes on their share of profits, even if no distribution takes place.

Management: In a GP, each partner has management authority.

'C' Corporation

Small-business owners rarely choose a corporation as their preferred business structure, but here is a little information to give you a point of reference. A 'C' Corporation has an unlimited number of shareholders. Officers, board members, and shareholders are not liable for company debts. The business entity is taxed on income, and shareholders are taxed on dividends. A 'C' Corporation is managed by the board of directors through its officers.

'S' Corporation

An 'S' Corporation is limited to one hundred shareholders. Resident alien shareholders, officers, board members, and shareholders are not liable for company debts. The tax structure is a pass-through taxation to shareholders (only one tax on company income), and the company is managed by the board of directors through its officers.

Again, don't allow yourself to be overwhelmed! You are accumulating information for the specific purpose of application. I guarantee that you understand business entity types at least 10 percent better than you did before you read the last few pages. If you still need assistance, consult with a trusted tax professional or with a credible business attorney (if you're in Texas, I happen to know a couple—hint, hint).

To determine the best entity type for you, consider:

1. The type of business you conduct

2. How you intend for that business to be managed

3. Tax implications

4. Personal liability

5. Initial investment and the need for additional or future investors

If you'd like some more information about business formation, as well as tips and tricks to better understand business entity types, feel free to visit our YouTube channel: JTL Attorneys.[11]

WHY YOU NEED A COMPANY AGREEMENT

Since limited liability companies (LLCs) are the most common business structure, we are going to talk about company agreements (sometimes referred to as operating agreements) in the context of an LLC. Many business owners, especially those who are sole proprietors or general partners, overlook the importance of a company agreement, but that can be a costly mistake.

A company agreement is a written contract that outlines how the business is going to be conducted. It includes the company's organizational information:

1. When and how the organization was formed

2. Membership of the company

3. Capital contributions—who and how much

4. Profit/loss allocation or distribution

5. How the business is managed

6. Indemnification and taxes

7. Financial setup and records

8. Transferring membership interests

9. Dissolution of the business

The company agreement is a contract that the business makes with itself with the expectation that the owners will comply with its terms. If there are any questions regarding how business ought to be conducted, what to do in the event of a dispute, or how to wrap up the business, the company agreement is the reference document. As we've mentioned, one of the major benefits of having an LLC is the limited liability. We will talk about reducing liability in the April chapter.

If you are married at the time of starting your business and live in a community property state such as Texas, you may want to include a spousal agreement that acknowledges that the business is your separate property.

Once you've signed your agreements and registered your company with the state, you may need to acquire an Employer Identification Number (EIN) with the IRS.

What Is an EIN and When Is It Required?

An EIN, or business tax ID, is a unique nine-digit number that you use when filing taxes for your business. The following types of businesses must obtain an EIN for tax purposes:

1. Any type of business entity with employees
2. Corporations and any entity taxed as a corporation
3. Multi-member LLCs

You must also obtain an EIN if:

1. You buy a business or inherit a business.
2. You have a solo 401(k) retirement plan.
3. You file for bankruptcy.

For a great guide regarding whether you need an EIN, visit the IRS page "Do You Need an EIN?" [12] If you answer "yes" to any of the questions listed, the website will take you to the page where you can easily apply for an EIN online. On a side note, only apply for an EIN through the IRS website. Many businesses will charge you to apply for an EIN. However, the IRS offers the application online for free and will immediately provide your EIN after you take a few minutes to answer some questions. We've seen many clients scammed by companies who claimed to be offering a couture service when, in fact, this service was available to our clients for free without them having to divulge sensitive data to a third-party organization.

Even if you are not legally required to have an EIN, there are some benefits associated with having one that may make it worth your while:

- An EIN speaks to the fact that you are a business entity. This is especially important if you intend to shield yourself from any liability that may be associated with your business and any potential tax penalties.

- When seeking work or partnering with other businesses, an EIN gives an air of professionalism, signaling that you take your business seriously.

- Most banking and financial institutions will require an EIN to open a business bank account.

- EINs can be used to establish and build business credit separate from your Social Security number and personal credit.

- If you ever intend to hire employees, it doesn't hurt to have an EIN now. There's no penalty associated with it, and it will save you time when you are ready to hire.

WHAT'S IN A NAME? EVERYTHING!

When brainstorming ideas for a new business name, I recommend thinking and praying on the following questions:

1. What name would describe the heart and vision of my business? (Example: Ceramic Wonders LLC)

2. Should I include my name within the name of my business? (Example: Sally Ceramics LLC)

3. Can I come up with a name that is memorable? (Example: Superhero Ceramics LLC)

4. Can I come up with a name that is a fun play on words? (Example: Seize the Clay Ceramics LLC)

Get creative and produce as many names as you can. Then narrow them down to your top five. Once you have your top five, conduct a name availability search with your Secretary of State. This process may narrow down your selections or, depending on how creative you were, may confirm that they are all still available for you to use. Next, we recommend going to the United States Patent and Trademark Office (USPTO) website and doing a search to see if the business name is available to trademark as well (which isn't required but may be desirable in the future with a logo, etc.).

Play around with how the business name looks on letterhead, business cards, and so forth. Will you associate it with a logo? How does it sound when your assistant answers the phone? Is it something that people can pronounce easily? Does that name have any sentimental value for you? Is it a name that is trendy but won't stand the test of time? Is it so common that it might be confused with other businesses in your area?

Your business name should mean something to you, and it should end up commanding respect with your clientele!

FINDING THE RIGHT BUSINESS PARTNER IS AKIN TO CHOOSING A SPOUSE

Choosing a business partner is as important, if not more important, than choosing a business type or even a business name. Whom you partner with in this venture will shape every decision you make going forward—not just what decisions you make, but how, when, and why you make them.

Selecting the right business partner is akin to choosing a spouse. Is this a person with whom you want to do life? Ebony and I can attest that there are weeks when we see one another more than we do our respective families. In fact, our families have grown close because our lives so often intersect—mostly when our kids giggle and run up and down the halls of our office building while we desperately try to outline the coming week's plan of action.

What should you look for in a business partner? First, I highly encourage you to begin with fasting and praying that God will lead you to the right person. We will talk more about fasting and prayer in the September chapter.

After you seek the Lord, I believe that the following questions will give you a suitable place to start:

1. Do my (potential) partner and I share the same vision, even if we have differing opinions on when and how that vision will manifest? Does my partner's passion match my passion, and vice versa?

2. Does my partner possess the character, integrity, and work ethic that the vision requires? As a self-check, if my partner were to work like I do, would much be accomplished? Would I be satisfied with my partner's effort, or would I find his or her work ethic lacking? Would it motivate and encourage me to want to do better and excel in areas where I might be lacking?

3. Is my partner responsible when it comes to managing money?

4. How supportive are my partner's spouse and/or family members of going into business?

5. Is there mutual respect and a path of honest communication between the two of us? Can I share ideas freely? Do I feel comfortable disagreeing or offering opposing viewpoints, or am I afraid that our relationship is too fragile to withstand a disagreement?

Considering the above questions is vital to a successful partnership. I also recommend that you do the work of self-evaluation to discover if you are the kind of person who would make a great business partner as well!

When Ebony and I first met, she was bravely making a name for herself as a solo practitioner, and I was entering my tenth year as an attorney for the great State of Texas. While I enjoyed my work and found elements of it rewarding, I had developed a deeper longing and passion to connect my legal profession with ministry. I wasn't sure what that would look like or if it would be a viable option for me as a single mom. Taking risks when it came to income and stability was not something I was keen to consider.

One day, a mutual friend introduced me to Ebony. He explained that she was a new attorney in the area, and that he was helping her make connections and build relationships with our peers. I don't remember anything life-changing happening between the two of us initially, but I do remember her smile and that over the several times we crossed paths after that, she often complimented my hair! We still laugh about that to this day.

In what I believe was providential, Ebony and I ended up working on a case together. As we organized our files and made small talk, we casually began a conversation about the various areas of law she practiced, one of which was church law. Church law? My interest was immediately piqued! I asked her more about this area of law, and she asked me if I'd ever considered going into private practice. Before we knew it, we were having dinner, spending time getting to know one another, and then fasting and praying about whether this was the right decision to make.

During that time, the Lord made it clear to me that He was not calling me to a place; He was calling me to a person. He was not necessarily calling me to private practice. He was calling me to Ebony.

Over time, as the Lord showed me what that looked like,

I gained confidence that Christ had called me to the right person, not necessarily a project or even a purpose at that time. God had a plan that incorporated both Ebony's and my gifts, passion, and calling. The underlying gifts and talents He had placed in each of us, combined with shared hopes and dreams (that we didn't even know we shared at first) began to surface as we spent more time together.

Through this God-centered relationship, our purpose was revealed, and projects started, but they were by-products of what Christ created by bringing us together. We have a collective "why" that allows us to push forward together when things don't always feel right. It's what reminded us of our goals when finances weren't adding up. It's what ignites our passion and rekindles our agape love for one another and for Christ. And it allows our business, our clients, and our families to be the blessed recipients of this confident assurance.

IT'S DUE SEASON!

Yet he did not waver through unbelief regarding the promise of God, but was strengthened in his faith and gave glory to God, being fully persuaded that God had power to do what he had promised.
—Romans 4:20–21 (NIV)

Nothing spurs us on more than a confident assurance in what we're doing and why we're doing it. A confident assurance in a God who created each of us with a purpose, abilities, and a calling. A confident assurance in the journey, complete with hills and valleys, successes and failures, quantum leaps and less than impressive bounds (or blips). Confidence is critical because our journeys won't always be a straight line. If your journey is a straight line, you're the exception!

In the midst of the challenges you will face, remembering your "what" and your "why" is non-negotiable, but even more important is the "who." The promises of God aren't powerful just because of the promises themselves. They are powerful because of the One who made them. Friend, if the desire to be an entrepreneur is one you cannot shake, it's likely that it was put there by God. Anything He calls you to do He will equip you to do. It's His promise to you, and He won't go back on His word.

Romans 4:20–21 refers to the unwavering belief of Abraham. This month, we are going to supplant Abraham in those verses and replace his name with ours. Then we are going to repeat these personalized verses to ourselves until they become our natural thinking process—until we believe.

Yet _____ did not waver through unbelief regarding the promise of God, but was strengthened in her faith and gave glory to God, being fully persuaded that God had the power to do what He had promised.[13]

January Notes

February:
Love Is in the "Aura"

Ebony Todd

To work without love is slavery.[14] —**Mother Teresa**

Love [verb]: the outward expression of unconditional care and extraordinary patience.

Love in business affects every area of operations, from quality to costs of services, from hiring and treatment of employees to customer relations and community outreach. In fact, I like to refer to business operations as a series of "love opportunities."

THE AUTHOR OF LOVE, PASSION, AND PURPOSE

The story of Jesus dying on the cross for us has been called the greatest *love* story of all time. One of the most popular depictions of this is the movie *Passion of the Christ*.[15] There are no vulgar sex scenes or even modest kissing scenes, yet the movie reenacted the most vulnerable, passionate, and desirable love of all.

Christ knew His purpose on earth: to show God's love by fulfilling His word. Jesus was very passionate about His purpose and didn't leave this earth until it was "finished" (John 19:30). In fact, Jesus fulfilled over three hundred prophecies during His thirty-three years of life!

As a CapitalMom and a godly entrepreneur, you should exude love and passion for your business. As the Word says, "Whatever you do, work heartily, as for the Lord and not for men" (Colossians 3:23 ESV).

We should all seek answers, through prayer and fasting, concerning God's purposes for our lives. No matter the assignment or path that God gives us or leads us to, we don't have to ask Him if we should proceed with love. He has already communicated very clearly that we are all required to love in everything we do!

WHAT DOES THE BIBLE REALLY SAY ABOUT LOVE?

Love is a verb and, therefore, requires action. But sometimes it's a noun that represents what you exude. Love should emanate from you, like an aura. The Christian definition of *love* is like no other! Found in 1 Corinthians 13:4–8 (which I've detailed below in the NIV), it's the perfect description of how God loves you and me. As believers, we should follow this model of love as well. Below, I've included an explanation of each word or phrase that Scripture uses to define love so that we can practically apply this godly love to every area of our lives, including our businesses.

"Love *is patient.*" We can accept or tolerate delays, problems, or suffering without becoming easily annoyed or unnecessarily anxious.

"Love *is kind.*" We have and show a friendly, generous, and considerate nature.

"Love ... *does not envy.*" We do not feel discontent or resentment related to someone else's possessions, qualities, or success.

"Love ... *does not boast.*" We do not speak with excessive pride and self-satisfaction about our achievements, possessions, or abilities.

"Love ... *is not proud.*" We accept constructive criticism and ask for help when we need it.

"Love ... *does not dishonor others.*" We are not rude, impolite, ill-mannered, abrupt, harsh, or impertinent.

"Love ... *is not self-seeking.*" We do not move in a self-centered, self-absorbed, or egotistical manner.

"Love ... *is not easily angered.*" We are not quick-tempered, hot-headed, irritable, or easily provoked.

"Love ... *keeps no record of wrongs.*" We don't hold the sins of others over their heads and become bitter or resentful, but rather demonstrate mercy and forgive others as Christ has forgiven us.

"Love *does not delight in evil.*" We do not take pleasure in foolishness, sinfulness, or immoral behavior, nor do we gloat over someone else's guilt or sin.

"Love ... *rejoices with the truth.*" We treasure truth, celebrate good behavior, and promote virtue.

"Love ... *always protects.*" We pray for, come to the aid of, support, and champion others.

"Love ... *always trusts.*" We stand ready to place our confidence in whom and what we love and always give the benefit of the doubt.

"Love ... *always hopes.*" We expect, anticipate, and look for God's goodness in others and in all our situations and circumstances.

"Love ... *always perseveres.*" We never give up, call it quits, or abandon love for others or for God when life or situations get difficult.

"Love *never fails.*" When we love God and love others, we can never fail in life.

FOUR LOVE PRINCIPLES

As you can see, First Corinthians gives us a clear strategic plan to accomplish love. But we also need to understand that apart from Christ, in our own strength, we cannot love this way. We must rely on the power of the Holy Spirit to transform the way we think and the way we love.

Here are four principles that, when understood and applied, are sure to edify others and intensify the "loving aura" in your personal life and your business.

Principle #1: Love Enables Prosperity

In the thirteenth century, German king Frederick II ordered an unnecessary experiment, commonly referred to as "Frederick's experiment." [16] He instructed his officials to take a number of babies from their mothers and put them in a special facility for the experiment. The king then ordered the nurses not to touch the infants affectionately or playfully, or even speak to them. The nurses were permitted only to feed, clean, and change the babies. King Frederick's purpose in the experiment was to determine what language the children would naturally develop if they weren't spoken to or touched.

King Frederick never found out the answer because every single baby died. We now label what happened to these poor children a "failure to thrive." One simply cannot prosper without love.

This concept applies to children and businesses alike.

Whether we're interacting with our children, employees, or customers, we should naturally exude the most basic of human needs: love. Otherwise, we could be setting up our businesses and children for failure.

Principle #2: Loving Your Business Emulates Parenting

Researchers from Aalto University in Helsinki, Finland, conducted a study that revealed that entrepreneurs love their businesses like their own children.[17] The researchers took brain scans of forty-two men while they were shown images of their companies and other businesses, as well as their kids and other people's children, respectively. They were asked questions regarding the emotions the photos evoked and the intensity of feelings such as love, fear, pride, joy, satisfaction, passion, disappointment, and sadness.

When examining the brain activity of the study participants, the scientists found that "entrepreneurial love is strikingly similar to paternal love" and that the parts of the brain that come alive when processing emotions, rewards, and social understanding occurred with both.[18]

I imagine that if the study had included CapitalMoms, there would have been comparable results. The maternal instinct of mothers makes us natural lovers and nurturers. This principle is not an argument that children and businesses should be loved in exactly the same manner. Nor does it substantiate placing your business before your family. This principle means that your business requires love, just as your children, pets, and even your home do. Shouldn't we steward with love all that God has entrusted us with?

Principle #3: Love Uses a "Heart Brain"

The heart is sometimes referred to as a "heart brain" because of its ability to sense things before the brain does.[19] In fact, the heart sends more signals to the brain than the brain sends to the heart.

Many business leaders consider love to be a worthy investment in their companies. Motivational speaker and author Steve Farber says that love is "an investment that produces both short- and long-term returns." [20] In his book about love and business, he states, "When love is part of an organization's framework, employees and customers feel genuinely valued and are more loyal, innovative, creative and inspired. A virtuous cycle occurs as well. Companies are more likely to produce products, services and experiences their customers will love. Customers will, in turn, reciprocate with their loyalty, referrals and, of course, their money. In other words, healthy employee relationships and customer retention, combined with the growth and abundance that aligns with love-based decisions, makes for a healthy and successful business." [21]

A CapitalMom shouldn't neglect the use of her brain to make business decisions, but it's also important to refer to your heart's desires when you're running a business.

Principle #4: Loving Your Business Requires Valuations

As entrepreneurs and, therefore, stewards of God's business, we show evidence of God within us by demonstrating love through our businesses—for example, in the products and services we provide, our attitude toward clients and clerks, and our diligence in researching. The list is lengthy. No matter the industry, we should not leave this earth without fervently exuding love.

Operating decisions can be daunting for a budding entrepreneur, especially when you're deciding what to charge for services and products. As a Christian mother who blesses others without pay on a regular basis, you may mistakenly believe that for your services to be "love opportunities," they need to be free. Don't get me wrong; it may be wise, reasonable, and effective to begin your business with market analysis and/or free sampling. However, it is equally wise, reasonable, and effective to expect competitive compensation.

Just because you're a Christian doesn't mean that you should charge less or take on all business that comes your way. In fact, because you love God, I believe that God is willing to bless and entrust you with more resources to do more for the benefit of God's people, including you and your family. He will also bless you with discernment to know when to take on new business and when to allow a consumer to find another accommodator. Referring someone to a competitor is simply another love opportunity.

When I initially opened my law firm, I discussed my fees

with my mother. Her reaction was epic. "That's high, Ebony!" I remember her saying. But I had a particular market that I was reaching out to, one comprised of serious clients who were able to afford legal services and desired to delegate tasks by outsourcing. When prospective clients (who can afford my fees) review my proposal, they're normally able to decide quickly. They value their time as well as mine and wish to tap into my competence, knowledge, and resources. That's my business market.

When we love our market, our business, and ourselves, we value our product or service accordingly. We also value love opportunities. This type of love may require us to turn down business at times. It may also require us to charge a price that's different from our competitors' prices. Either way, our stewardship should reflect love.

Loving something or someone requires the enabling of purpose and prosperity. When you love God's people, you will exemplify love to your business. This requires you to love:

- your clients or customers,
- your employees,
- yourself, and others.

You Had Me at Hello: Loving Your Customers

Hopefully, by now you know that your aura of love should be so palpable that your customers feel it when you greet them. Loving customers doesn't mean that you make any physical contact with them (except for professions in which physical contact is permissible or required, such as nursing). Rather, it entails listening to your customers' needs and accommodating them as appropriate. Provide the best services or products that you can without sacrificing other valuable people, including yourself, in the process.

Loving your customers or clients doesn't mean that the customer is always right. The attorney in me has always despised that phrase. Although I realize the intent behind the adage, I don't believe that it properly prepares a professional to manage each specific situation. In fact, an upset and unsatisfied customer may simply need to be recognized and heard.

I once had a dental appointment that I believed was to begin a procedure, but I learned upon arrival that it was a preparatory appointment. I was very aggravated. This was my third or fourth appointment, and each time I had an appointment at this trusted and prestigious dental office, I had to drive almost two hours and lose an entire day of work as well as coordinate my sons' pickup from school. (At the time, my husband was deployed, and we weren't even considering having a third child.) My demeanor changed immediately, and I walked out of the dental office. I know—dramatic.

Once I made it to my vehicle, I called my mom (because that's what you do when you're upset and need to hear a reasonable voice). My mother very calmly explained to me how important it was that I didn't upset the people responsible for caring for my mouth.

I walked back into the dental office and asked to speak with a dentist. I told the dentist my concerns, and he was immediately apologetic and promised that he wanted me to have a good experience. He was sorry that the procedural process had not been explained to me in an appropriate way, but he assured me that the preparatory appointments were important.

I felt relieved after speaking to him. I felt loved. I didn't get what I wanted (which was to never have to return!), but I left that office feeling heard and valued.

Loving your customers will require you to identify their purpose of collaborating with you and then make it your mission to fulfill that purpose diligently. Each customer should leave your business more prosperous than when he or she came in—whether this means being more informed, more relaxed, more beautiful, more equipped, more satisfied, or having acquired more resources to be successful. At times, you may have bad customers, days, and experiences, but your goal should always be to love in a way that reflects God's love and enables your customers' purpose and prosperity.

Legally Showing Your Clients or Customers Love

As an attorney, I have the job of thinking of the worst-case scenario. We call this "issue spotting." I'm constantly trying to prevent terrible things from happening to my clients.

One of the worst-case scenarios business owners must address is disputes. At times, a client may immediately want to escalate the dispute by suing. Some spiritual leaders find it sinful to sue one another. If you agree, you may want to consider Alternative Dispute Resolutions, such as arbitration, mediation, and negotiation. (We will discuss these options in more detail in the November chapter.)

As a Christian, you may want to take it a step further and include terms of your agreements that require a Christian mediator, arbiter, and/or negotiator. You may also consider a Christian Conciliation clause in your agreements, and you could employ entities such as Peacemaker Ministries or the Institute for Christian Conciliation to resolve your issues.

Another way to show your clients and customers love legally is to abstain from false advertisement, the marketing of your services or products using misleading or untrue information. Besides this being self-seeking, it is also illegal to advertise falsely. Be sure to choose your words carefully when advertising your products and show love for others by not misleading them or stating outright lies.

Taking these steps is a way to show God's love to people through your actions.

HUGS AND POLICIES: LOVING YOUR EMPLOYEES

How your employees feel can either positively or negatively affect the "aura" of your business. When your employees feel loved, your business wins! To love an employee requires much more time and attention than needed with customers. In most businesses, appropriate relationships can be fostered with employees. The exception to this is large corporations, in which owners and leaders may not know or relate to every employee, yet we are now seeing more corporations invest in their employees in areas such as college tuition, incentives, and other benefits.

In 2015, Dan Price of Gravity Payments increased all 120 of his employees' salaries and, in doing so, took a 90 percent pay decrease of his own $1 million salary. In his effort to make each employee's minimum annual salary $70,000 by 2024, he took another pay cut in 2019. He has inspired other business leaders to do the same. I'm sure there are people who think that he's crazy, but *I think* that he loves his employees, loves what he does, and certainly loves his business. His actions will surely result in employee retention and loyalty, which will, in turn, result in business growth and assuredly earn him more than the original salary amount.

As a small-business owner, you may choose to host employee appreciation days on which you purchase lunch, let your employees off early (paid time off), and spend quality time with each employee. You could invite their families to an appreciation day as well. If you don't have the resources for an event, you could show your appreciation with simple thank-you cards and gift cards. (We'll cover the subject of gratitude in the November chapter). No matter the gesture, if it is thoughtful and genuine, your employees will feel appreciated and, hopefully, loved.

In an effort to build a sense of family at work (if that's a goal of yours), you may consider introducing your employees to your family. Having time with your employees and family together allows your employees to see your family dynamic and could make them feel more like family. It also shows them that you value family time.

Legally Showing Employees Love

There are also preventative law measures through which you can show love to your company. Before we address those measures, let's define *preventative law*. Preventative laws are actionable steps taken to prevent issues, lawsuits, and conflicts. When showing love to your employees, you should have written policies. These policies, when properly drafted and consistently followed, prevent employees from feeling treated unfairly, which in turn may prevent unemployment claims. It can also decrease the risk of misunderstandings and misconduct.

Consider the following legal actions of love:

1. Bereavement policies. Having a policy in place for employees if a family member or friend dies can be a testament to your personal values. Whether your company permits time off (paid or unpaid) to grieve, it should be according to what you can afford and consistent for all employees.

2. Providing information concerning laws that affect employees, such as the Families First Coronavirus Response Act. For reasons related to COVID-19, the Families First Coronavirus Response Act required certain employers to provide employees with paid sick leave or expanded medical and family leave. Most small businesses were exempt from the requirement based on their companies' viability. Nonetheless, the companies required to provide the leave best showed their employees love by being forthcoming with the information and not trying to hide their legal obligations. Consider how being forthcoming with information in your small business can show love.

3. Maintaining Workman's Compensation Insurance (also called "workman's comp"). Workman's comp is a special type of insurance that protects businesses and employees from monetary loss in the event that an employee is sick or hurt on the job. Even if workman's comp isn't required in your state, maintaining it can reflect love and appreciation for your employees.

There are a host of other ways to show your employees love, such as training them, giving them feedback, remaining flexible, and so much more. Be creative in how you show your employees love on a regular basis.

I Heart You: Loving Yourself and Others

How you treat yourself and others can directly impact your aura and how you love your clients and employees. Just as it's important for you to love your children, it's equally important for you to love yourself and other individuals in your life, such as business partners, your spouse, and your friends.

Loving Yourself

I recently complimented one of my friends on her self-love because she always managed to groom herself in ways that gave the appearance that she loved and cared about herself. She immediately corrected me by reminding me that there is a difference between *self-care* and *self-love*. Although she always made time for grooming herself, she often struggled with loving herself. I felt sad that someone I admired so much could struggle with self-love. It also enlightened me that it's not enough for us, as women, to get our nails done or to do our hair to show ourselves love.

Showing myself love these days requires me to wake up before my husband and children to enjoy quiet time with the Lord, praying and reading the Word. Other times, it looks like a midday nap to catch up on sleep lost during the week of "Wonder-woman-ing." Recently, loving myself has included having a writing retreat with my business partner to draft the book of my dreams, without guilt that I've left my children at home with dad during their spring break! What it means to love myself is not the same from day to day, but I try to give love to myself daily—and so should you!

Loving Others

I make every effort to show my business partner, Shai, love as well. One of my favorite books is *The Five Love Languages* by Gary Chapman.[22] If you've never read it, I encourage you to buy a copy. But when Shai revealed to me that she couldn't relate to any of the five love languages of gift giving, words of affirmation, quality time, physical touch, or acts of service, I felt like a tire losing air. This totally baffled me.

I thought, *"How can I express love in a way that resonates with her?"*

My resolve led me to combine all five love languages for her. I prayed that somehow the combination of all five would make her feel loved. On a regular basis, you will find me buying her flowers, writing cards with affirmations, hugging her, and trying to assist her with cases and clients. I don't force it, but I am deliberate.

My husband, James, on the other hand, knows for certain that his love languages are words of affirmation and quality time. As a natural encourager and a lover of physical touch, I find that these two come easily for me. That could be the reason we pair well. We make a concerted effort to have pillow talk nightly, watch a movie after our children are in bed (the movie may be watching me), and escape from "escape rooms" regularly.

I'm also sensitive to the love languages of my children.

Our eldest, whom we call Jet, is super caring and loving. As far as love languages go, he's a lot like me. He loves gifts and physical touch. Our middle son, whom we call Major, is a fantastic anomaly of our family. We're still trying to figure him out at the tender age of five, but because he hardly cares what I say and prefers not to be touched, he's mostly into playtime (quality time) for now. Our youngest daughter, whom we call 7, is still a baby, but I can already tell that she's a no-nonsense child. She may be a little harder to figure out, like her Aunt Shai.

Nonetheless, like all other children, they need time with mommy and have time to evolve. I try to be flexible and mindful that they are growing and maturing, so what they need may change. Most importantly, I give them my time. Kerwin Rae, a business strategist, coach, and author, reminds us not to get so busy building or businesses that we neglect quality time with our kids: "The way your kids spell love is T-I-M-E." [23]

Loving Your Competitors

At the risk of sounding counterintuitive, I want to emphasize that just as we are to love our families and our neighbors, we should also love our competitors. I personally trust that God will bring the clients that are specifically for my business. There isn't anything another competitor can do to stop what God has for me. Something I do may delay it or prevent me from accomplishing a goal, but I doubt that another person's actions can prevent God's blessings in my life. With that mindset, I make every effort to enable competition to succeed.

There's a moving story in *Business by the Book* by Larry Burkett.[24] It's about a man named Will who epitomized loving his competitor, in this case a former employee whom he had groomed to become the president of his company. After learning that his competitor was facing several lawsuits because of a design flaw in his product, Will purchased his competitor's product, fixed it, and divulged the defect and how to fix it to his competitor. Now, that's love!

Get to know your competitors, not just for marketing purposes, but so you can love them and even direct business to them when it's appropriate to do so. There are times when I'm approached about business litigation and, although I am a business law attorney, I'm a mother first, so I kindly refer some litigation to other business law attorneys who are equipped to handle the cases. I love when competitors to whom I refer potential clients refer clientele to me, because I know that they are showing our business love in return.

Legally Showing Yourself

Loving yourself requires you to protect yourself and your property. You may do so legally by investing in protecting your company's intellectual property. Intellectual property—trademarks, copyright, patents, and trade secrets—is discussed in more detail in the April chapter. Having a basic understanding of intellectual property will empower you to know when it's appropriate to invest in further protections for your company's assets, which is a sure sign of love.

IT'S DUE SEASON!

In this chapter, we explored the concept of love according to the original source and discussed how four principles of love relate to mompreneurs. We also found practical ways to express love for our businesses, customers, clients, employees, partners, family, and competitors.

Although there isn't an expectation for CapitalMoms to be doormats, we should maintain the utmost integrity and character while personifying love daily. Be mindful of the needs of individuals in your life and be deliberate with your love. It benefits you and your business when you actively show love to everyone in your life, including yourself. Don't allow your drive to succeed in business to inhibit your ability and willingness to love others. Instead, allow it to enable and promote your aura of love.

As women of God, we should epitomize love. Below you'll find an affirmation that will help you to grow in your embodiment and demonstration of love. You'll note that I've taken lines from the Bible, such as "Love is patient," and re-written them from your perspective ("I am patient").

In the first line below, replace the blank line with a reference to "myself," "my child(ren)," "my spouse," "my friends," "my business partner," "my employees," "my customers/clients," and/or "my business." Then recite the following affirmation at least once a day for the following month.

I am patient. I value _____ enough to give them the attention and time they require and deserve.

I am kind. I want what's best for others.

I do not envy. I want others to have what God has for them and appreciate the stewardship required for their individual gifts and talents.

I do not boast. I appreciate my blessings and do not feel the need to share with the intent to brag or to be self-important.

I am not proud. I am wise enough to know that I cannot do life without assistance.

I am not rude. I respond with love.

I am not self-seeking. I understand that my gifts, talents, and passions have been given to me with the expectation of stewardship. I will serve not only for my own benefit, but for the benefit of others as well.

I am not easily angered. I respond thoughtfully to negative actions, news, and expressions.

I keep no record of wrongs. I understand that I make mistakes as well, and I hope that my mistakes will be forgiven by others.

I do not delight in evil but rejoice with the truth. I want God's will to prevail.

I protect my family, my business, my reputation, and my integrity.

I trust God in my ventures.

I hope to please God and enable my legacy.

I will persevere.
With God, I never fail.

February Notes

PART TWO: SPRING

March:

How to Endure the Unexpected

Shinia Lambert

If you can't, you must. If you must, you can.[25]
—Tony Robbins

Madness [noun]: extremely foolish behavior; a state of frenzied or chaotic activity.[26]

Wow. Can you relate to the above definition? I sure can, and I'm quite sure that you can, too! We could just sit here and reread it a few times and feel the weight of its truth sink into our bones. Honestly, I wish that we could grab a cup of coffee and talk each other's heads off about how we relate to the feelings of sheer madness in life. *A state of frenzied or chaotic activity*—are you kidding me? This is my life! "Hello, my name is Frenzied and Chaotic. Nice to meet you."

When the Unexpected Occurs

I don't know about you, but if I never hear the words *pandemic, pivot,* or *unprecedented* again, it will be too soon! Nevertheless, COVID-19 and its effects on our families and businesses cannot be ignored when we're talking about the unexpected.

What do you do when you're balancing—or trying desperately to balance—a healthy home life and a successful business amid the various challenges and outright disappointments that you face every single day? How do you maintain a sense of normalcy when the unexpected is always sneaking its unwanted head into your business, such as your child Zoombombing your client video calls? Is there something we all can do to prepare ourselves for the unexpected so that we can successfully navigate our way through uncharted waters? And can we do this while continuing to be the amazing mothers, wives, and contributors to society that we desire to be?

Brigid Schulte and Stavroula Pabst, in their article "Combating Burnout as a Single Working Parent," wrote, "Women, regardless of their marital status, have borne the brunt of childcare and homeschooling in the pandemic. It's part of why 2.3 million women have been forced out of the workforce." [27]

Trying to balance motherhood, home life, and business is an area both Ebony and I understand personally and speak about. When COVID-19 hit the globe in 2020, it swept through our nation, affecting everyone from young to old and everything from home to business. No one had clear answers on what to do or how to do it! As mothers trying to keep our families safe as well as continue to function at work, we found ourselves inundated with fear and on information overload. To say that we were overwhelmed is an understatement.

While the world scrambled to face this abrupt interruption, crowds swarmed local stores, gathering necessities and preparing for the worst. As mompreneurs, we were not only concerned about what a pandemic meant personally for us and our families, but also what a shutdown would mean for our business. Never in the history of my life did a regular 9-to-5 job seem so attractive.

As various industries tried to offset a disruption of production and provision of services, most allowed employees to work from home, while small-business owners were left to create a new normal. Many businesses that operated solely out of brick-and-mortar stores or offered in-person services, such as spas and restaurants, were forced to close down temporarily. When could we reopen? Who knew? Nobody knew! Some business owners were so determined to keep their doors open that they resisted the shutdown, willing to face severe, legal consequences.

It was terrifying to say the least and a challenge for even the most devoted believer. Where did this come from? Why did it happen? Why weren't we warned? And what were we all supposed to do now?

OUR OWN APPROACH TO THE UNEXPECTED

When the school year began in Fall 2020 in our state of Texas, parents had to make the decision whether to send their kids to school (with new mask and PPE protocols in place) or allow their children to participate in virtual learning. Like all other mompreneurs, Ebony and I had to figure out what was best for our families and how that decision would affect the way we do business. I know that we touched on this in the January chapter, but I cannot emphasize enough just how important it is to pray about whom you choose as your business partner. COVID-19 presented us with a perfect example of how life, family, and business intersect, sometimes unexpectedly.

Ebony and I had a transparent and vulnerable conversation with each other. For me, it was clear that I needed my son to be with me in a virtual learning environment. Not only did it help to assuage my anxiety for him, but it also made it safer for me not to catch the virus since I have asthma and often suffer from upper respiratory infections—two of the pre-existing conditions that authorities warned could make COVID-19 a killer diagnosis. In addition, as my own boss, I now had the luxury of having my son with me, a choice I never could have made were I still working a traditional 9-to-5 job. Ebony completely supported my decision and went a step further, suggesting that I work one day a week from home to give my son a break from the office environment.

While all of this was happening, Ebony's husband, James, deployed, and she was managing to raise two young (albeit amazing) boys on her own, with some help from family. For Ebony, making the decision to send her children back to school took more consideration than simply what was convenient for her. There was nothing easy about having to abide by the plethora of new protocols, arranging for school drop-off and pickup, monitoring her children's health, and limiting interaction with others. There were several factors for her to consider—not only, but especially, her mental health. My business partner would be quick to tell you that she excels when working in silence or playing classical music, and how many of us can say that our kids allow us that opportunity, especially when we have multiple children and there's an age difference?

Our decisions equally reflected the totality of the circumstances, including what we knew to be true about ourselves and what we needed mentally to be able to continue to excel as entrepreneurs. The important part is that, although we were led to different decisions, we loved and supported one another enough to allow each other to do what we believed to be best. And that, my friend, made all the difference.

As women, we are taught that sacrifice equates to love. Yet it seems that we are the ones doing all the forfeiting, and at the end of the day, we are truly sacrificing ourselves. That's not what God intended. Nowhere is there a blueprint that requires you to be less.

Still, I sometimes wrestle with this. As a single mother, I often struggle with prioritizing my own needs because, although no one specifically tells me that my child must come first at all times and in all things, I often feel guilty for wanting "alone time," for wanting more autonomy, for vacationing alone, and so forth. I'm still working through this. I've found that what helps to release me from those feelings of guilt is reminding myself that I'm only as good to my son as I am to myself. If I'm stressed, burned out, and resentful, I'm not able to give my optimal self to him or to my business.

I'm not talking about pride. The Bible says that God hates pride (Proverbs 8:13). I'm also not talking about selfishness, which is not attractive. What I'm saying is that valuing yourself as an individual with your own hopes, desires, and dreams is not the antithesis to being a great wife and/or mother!

After Ebony and I united regarding how we would manage our families during this time, we were then free to focus on how we would do business. We couldn't afford to shut down altogether, and thank God, we never felt the pressure to do so. Yet, with restrictions on which businesses could operate and how, we knew that adjustments would need to be made to continue to attract new clients, consult with them, and provide traditional trial representation.

So adjust we did. We began offering phone and virtual consultations. Clients loved the opportunity to interact with us from the comfort of their own homes or businesses. COVID-19 caused us to explore options that we'd never considered because they didn't seem necessary. Once we realized that virtual consultations were often preferred, it allowed us to broaden our playing field and consult with clients no matter where they were geographically in the state. Virtual consultations opened a new market for us!

Are we grateful for COVID-19? Clearly not. But are we

grateful that we were forced to explore new options to do business that we might have otherwise missed? Absolutely.

GOD PROVIDES A WAY
THROUGH THE UNEXPECTED

Do you need encouragement to trust God with something you have never seen, an unexpected trial, event, or circumstance that seemed to come out of nowhere?

Think about Noah for a moment (Genesis 6). He planned for the future with no blueprint to follow other than the voice of his God. Imagine being told by God to build an ark the size of a campus yet having no idea what an ark was! Imagine being told that the ark would keep your family safe while God flooded the entire earth with torrential rain for forty days and nights. Oh, did I mention that Noah, along with the rest of the earth's inhabitants, had never seen rain? Noah was building something he had never seen for something that had never happened before. Genesis 6:22 reads, "And Noah did this. He did everything that God had commanded him" (CSB).

COVID-19 was our personal flood, and virtual consulting and the various other adjustments we were called to make were our ark. It wasn't glamorous, but we were desperate to trust God in circumstances we could never have foreseen, and He revealed a way for us to escape and prosper, despite the chaos all around us!

SHOWER YOURSELF WITH SOME GRACE

This book is a place to learn about business avenues you might not have considered and no one has bothered to tell you about before. It is our passion to see women excel in business while also excelling at home, so we're not hiding the ball here. You're allowed to make mistakes. You're allowed to fail outright at something. Neither mistakes nor failure diminishes you or your calling. So give yourself some grace because the Lord certainly showers His grace upon you!

Give yourself permission to say "no" to certain things that are not really yours to carry right now. Force yourself to delay or delegate certain things that are not your primary mission in this moment. In doing so, you'll find that every "yes" comes with a whole lot more freedom and fulfillment.

Dr. Lissa Rankin wrote, "It seems to me that too many of us wear busyness as a badge of honor. I'm busy, therefore I'm important and valuable, therefore I'm worthy. And if I'm not busy, forget it. I don't matter." [28]

There are some dangers present when we are not intentional about giving ourselves grace and we allow productivity to steer us toward perfectionism. First, we compare ourselves to others and feel negative about ourselves because we are choosing to allow others' success to magnify our perceived shortcomings.

Second, we allow ourselves to believe the lie that we must always have it all together. We shy away from asking for much-needed help, because we think that seeking or accepting help means that we are "less than" or not capable when all it actually means is that we need some help!

Last but not least, we allow ourselves to be overwhelmed because we refuse to relinquish control. This leads to us feeling frustrated and depleted instead of learning to trust others and delegate responsibilities to those whose job it is to manage them.

Refuse to take on this yoke that God didn't give you! Give yourself grace. Stop comparing yourself to others, ask for help when you need it, and relinquish control to others in areas where they are knowledgeable and gifted. You will find that when you do these things, your life and business will be far more successful.

WHEN THE UNEXPECTED IS PREDICTABLE

Okay, you just read the title of this section, and I know what you're thinking. If something is unexpected, how can it be predictable at the same time? Before you come to the conclusion that I've completely lost my mind, let me give you some examples of what I mean. There are times in life when we face unexpected challenges or trials that, in hindsight, we should have seen coming. If we spend most of our lives eating poorly, never going to the doctor, and living an unhealthy lifestyle, should we really be surprised by the health challenges we may face?

There is only one kind of shock worse than the totally un-expected: the expected for which one has refused to pre-pare.[29]

—Mary Renault

Simply put, unexpected challenges and hardships can come our way because they are the outcome of wrong choices, improper planning and preparation, or taking the easy way out, which never results in an easy outcome.

As moms, we teach our kids that their choices and deci-sions can bear certain consequences (or outcomes, which often sounds more gracious). The same is true for adults.

For example, we have known business owners who didn't get help with contracts. They signed a binding document without reading or even understanding the terms. Then, a couple of years into their business, they were hit with a mas-sive increase in their rent because the triple net clause in their lease was in effect.

One client came to us in this exact situation. His world turned upside down because his office expenses suddenly tri-pled—and I don't mean by a few dollars; we're talking a five-digit increase! This unexpected turn of events threw him into chaos and threatened his livelihood. The reality of his situa-tion was that if he had understood the terms of his lease or at least had gotten help from an attorney on the contract, he would not have faced this unexpected situation. The increase was part of his contract, but he didn't realize that fact. Sadly, these types of unexpected situations happen all the time. What is sadder is that they don't have to.

The benefit of having legal counsel on your team is the opportunity to have someone review your documents and contracts, help you to weigh your options, and let you know the consequences if you fail to fulfill your obligations. The time to do all of this is *before* you sign the contract! You may not know the law, but courts do expect you to abide by it. Ignorance is not a defense.

The kind of attorneys you want on your team are those who value and esteem preventative law, attorneys who will expend their effort on the front end to make sure that your contracts are airtight and that you have built-in protections in the event that something goes wrong further down the line. A great attorney will foresee contractual pitfalls that you're not familiar with and will have access to resources that might give you a better alternative when you're entering negotiations.

Far too often, business owners utilize attorneys in the opposite order, only getting them involved after something has gone wrong. Remember that "an ounce of prevention is worth a pound of cure." If you're currently reviewing an offer, participating in a negotiation, or drafting a contract from scratch, it's time to consider hiring an attorney.

WHEN IS THE RIGHT TIME TO HIRE AN ATTORNEY?

Whether and when you hire an attorney has more to do with where you are mentally in the process of starting and growing your business than any other factor. There are clear indications that you are *not* ready to hire an attorney. Yep, I just said that! Here's how you know that you *are* ready:

- You understand the value of hiring an attorney.

- You trust the attorney whom you're considering hiring.

- You are not willing to settle for less than credible service solely because you believe that it's all you can afford.

As practicing attorneys in business law, we have had a myriad of clients, some of whom were completely ready to get their business started and were already going in the right direction. They saw hiring an attorney team as the next critical step in their business efforts, and they not only envisioned the kind of results they wanted to see, but were also willing to put in the work needed to get those results.

On the other hand, we have had clients who hired an attorney because they knew that was what they *should* be doing, but they were not prepared mentally, or sometimes even financially, for the responsibility of having someone else lead them. What do I mean by that?

The attorney–client relationship often has the outward appearance of being stoic and cold because you're working on paperwork, contracts, and intellectual property. But for people who are truly enthusiastic about their business and vision—and are more than likely investing their hard-earned money in it—the attorney–client relationship is not cold. If you have a good attorney, he or she will be invested in your business and your vision as well. In fact, when you combine your passion for your business with someone who believes in you and wants to see you succeed, it becomes a relationship that is so much more than paperwork.

The relationship you have with your attorney needs to be grounded in an innate level of trust. We have had situations in which our ability to assist clients was hindered because no matter how sound our counsel was, they wouldn't relinquish control. Failure to relinquish control is usually a sign of fear, which is the result of a lack of trust. If you cannot trust the person you're paying to represent your best interests, then it's time to revisit whether you're truly ready for an attorney.

Believe it or not, there are costs associated with having an attorney. I know that sounds strange for me to say, because who doesn't know that? But you would be amazed at how many potential clients come into our office with a laundry list of services they're interested in and then wrap up by saying, "Well, right now I don't have any money."

It's one thing to go to a consultation with the intention of gathering information and getting an idea of a next step. That's a legitimate outlook and usually shows that the person is preparing to reach that next step of hiring an attorney. But to consult with an attorney with an expectation that you want him or her to perform a service, yet you have no means to pay for that service, is both insulting and a waste of everyone's time. Having an attorney requires being financially ready to hire one.

Ebony and I cannot emphasize enough how important it

is to be ready to invest in your business if you want to see your business grow. As small-business owners ourselves, we understand how difficult that can be, but one of the hardest lessons we had to learn—and learn fast—was that you need to spend money to make money.

Investing in a solid legal team is one of the best investments you can make. I'm quite sure that you don't have dreams of going into business because you like paperwork, enjoy reviewing contracts or leases, and want to negotiate the terms of your next business deal. You have a product, a service, a talent, a gift that you want to market and share with the world. So if you are in the beginning stages of your business, we strongly recommend that one of your budget items be legal counsel.

When it comes to hiring an attorney, you need to ask yourself these three questions:

- Am I mentally prepared to entrust my business needs to someone else?

- Am I financially prepared to be responsible for hiring an attorney?

- Am I professionally prepared to invest in myself to see my business grow?

Let me be clear. I don't know any business owners who are willing to abdicate their responsibility and relinquish all control. But I do know smart business owners who acknowledge their strengths and have learned to entrust and delegate tasks to others gifted in areas that the business owners are not. Plus, in the interim, you get to support other businesses. In practical terms, that might look something like this:

- Acknowledging that your math teacher in high school was right and you will need to use math in real life, you hire a seasoned bookkeeper to track your expenses and assist with budgeting.

- Instead of using your best working hours answering the phone or greeting walk-ins, you hire a college student to work as your administrative assistant. It frees up your time and allows the student to add the experience to his or her résumé.

- Instead of spending hours researching how to design a website, you outsource it to someone who designs great websites and whose work you admire.

Starting your business involves demanding work and a great deal of preparation and planning. But your gifts and talents, your vision and passion, your faith, and your calling will catapult you to the place you desire to be.

PREPARE, PLAN, AND EXPECT THE UNEXPECTED!

Pray for God's wisdom and build a solid foundation for your business. Prepare, plan, and yes, expect the unexpected! When you trust in God's presence and guidance and you put in the hard work of building a firm foundation, you will find that when the unexpected comes your way, you will not only rise to the challenge, but will find new opportunities and pathways to enrich your business and prosper.

I have added the following definitions of terms for contracts to help you as you prepare and plan for the launch of your business.

LEGAL RESOURCES REGARDING CONTRACT TERMS

Arbitration Clause: provides Alternative Dispute Resolution. It requires that parties attempt to resolve their matters through an arbitration process. The goal is to avoid the cost of litigation.

Common Area Maintenance (CAM): an additional rental expense that is intended to cover expenses involved with shared areas. CAM makes up one of the nets in triple net (NNN). Common area is any space that is used by more than one tenant, a space to which no one tenant has exclusive access. All tenants share the expense to maintain that common space. It is important when reviewing a lease to be sure that you are not considering only the cost of the monthly rent, but also any additional expenses, such as CAM.

Disclaimers: clauses or statements included in a contract to try to minimize or diminish risk liability. You will typically see these relating to goods. A seller or manufacturer may deny responsibility for the effectiveness of their products, making no promises regarding how well the products will perform and produce results.

Indemnification Clause: To indemnify someone means to compensate him or her for harm or loss. In a contract, this clause serves to compensate a party for harm or loss that arises as the result of the other party's actions or omissions.

Noncompete Clause: outlines an agreement that the signing party contracts not to compete with the other. These clauses can be customized to fit the market, niche, and type of business in which you are engaged. The noncompete can state how long a party may be prevented from competing and/or a radius in which the party cannot compete. The clause cannot be unreasonable or overly burdensome to the extent that it would reduce someone's ability to maintain a livelihood, but it can protect your business from being exploited by individuals who were once employees, partners, or even independent contractors.

Nondisclosure: This is more of a separate agreement versus a clause in a contract. The parties agree that any information that has been disclosed and shared with one another as a part of doing business will remain confidential and will not be shared, without permission, with outside parties. Nondisclosure agreements are particularly important when you are shopping for opportunities and negotiating contracts. Imagine presenting to five companies about your innovative solution to increasing diversity in their workplace and providing samples of your workbooks and computer courses, all without anyone signing a nondisclosure. Those materials may be up for grabs!

Notice Clause: This is a part of the contract that may seem minor but is extremely important. This portion lays out where and how parties are to contact and communicate with one another. Notices of intent to vacate premises, intent to terminate the contract, or allegations of a breach must be sent not only within a certain time frame, but also to a specific place or person of contact.

Triple Net (NNN): is a term in a commercial lease agreement that means the tenant agrees to pay three expenses associated with the property: (1) real estate taxes, (2) building insurance, and (3) shared area maintenance. Be diligent in reviewing your lease or having an attorney review it to discover whether these "hidden" expenses are included in your lease.

IT'S DUE SEASON!

Here are some important points to remember from this chapter:

- Valuing yourself as an individual with your own hopes, desires, and dreams is not the antithesis to being a great wife and/or mother.

- When the unexpected hits your life and your business, don't panic. Learn to adjust, adapt, and pursue creative options to keep on keeping on.

- Trust God amid the unexpected and He will lead you through to the other side.

- You are allowed to make mistakes and even to fail outright at something. Neither mistakes nor failure diminishes you or your calling. So give yourself some grace because the Lord certainly showers His grace upon you!

- Don't cheat yourself or your business. Prevent the predictable type of unexpected situation from happening by investing in preventive law before you sign a contract, agreement, or lease.

- Know when to say "no," when to say "yes," and when to relinquish control!

March Notes

April:
Spring Cleaning and
Protecting Your Gift

Ebony Todd

The objective of cleaning is not just to clean, but to feel happiness living within that environment.[30]
—Marie Kondo

Clean [verb]: the act of removing what does not belong on a person, place, or thing.

I find it amusing that I would author the chapter concerning cleanliness. Not that I am disgusting or filthy, but I can be a bit junky at times. Even now, as I look around my desk, I see books scattered and stacked, a pen next to a couple of unnecessary cell phones, snacks, and a few other things surrounding my laptop. Nonetheless, I've learned the value of organization to achieve cleanliness. And where I lack, I delegate.

In fact, I've hired a housekeeping service to clean my home twice a month. I've noticed the change in my personal demeanor when my home is nice and tidy. I also have increased productivity when my space at work is organized, and I know where I can quickly find items I need.

The same principles can be applied to my heart. I feel much better when I know that I'm doing the right thing, when I have repented after doing the wrong thing, and when I practice what I preach.

As a busy mother and entrepreneur—a CapitalMom!— it's important for me to practice cleanliness at my place of business and within my heart and to delegate as appropriate. In this chapter (month), we will explore the significance of business cleanliness, organization, delegation, and protection.

PHYSICAL CLEANLINESS AND PRODUCTIVITY

The pandemic forced us all to focus on the importance of maintaining sanitary and safe work conditions for employees and customers. Although disinfecting everything is at the forefront of our minds now, it has always been important to maintain cleanliness.

You might have heard the maxim "cleanliness is next to godliness." A friend of mine used to be told by her mother that the saying was in the Bible. I can still remember when my friend called me to tell me, with a tinge of aggravation in her voice, that she had read the entire Holy Bible and nowhere did it say those words! As a result, I learned online that it was John Wesley, the founder of the Methodist church, who cemented those words in the world. Whether it's in the Bible or not, I do believe that there's powerful truth in the idea that "cleanliness is next to godliness."

Research has shown that women with messy homes, unfinished projects, and cluttered spaces are more likely to be depressed and fatigued, as well as have increased levels of cortisol, the stress hormone that triggers our bodies' home alarm systems when too high.[31] Another research study found that cluttered and messy spaces cause us to be visually overstimulated, which results in a lack of focus and efficiency.[32]

Maintaining a clean and sanitary space isn't simply good for your personal well-being; it may also prevent unnecessary litigation. During the pandemic, many businesses faced litigation by their employees for maintaining unsafe working conditions and for a lack of Personal Protective Equipment (PPE). Nursing homes, restaurants, meat processing companies, shopping centers, and many more were sued due to their lack of sanitation practices and/or PPE.

Physical cleanliness affects our productivity, especially when it comes to organization. In 1 Corinthians 14:40, Paul wrote to the church in Corinth that they should "be sure that everything is done properly and in order" (NLT). Paul went on to instruct the church regarding how to organize public worship in a way that ministers to those who are listening, making sure that clutter did not interfere with the message.

Does your clutter affect how you do business? Does it affect how you think? Does it affect your clientele?

Your cleanliness and productivity hinge on your level of attention to detail. Reading through the Bible, you'll find many scriptures that illustrate God's preference for organization and attention to detail. For example:

- God commanded Noah to construct a large boat and fill it with animals (Genesis 6:14–22). He gave Noah exact specifications, including the type and measurements of materials.

- The Lord instructed Moses how to construct the tabernacle and the Ark of the Covenant (Exodus 25). Again, God gave specific measurements and types of materials to use.

- Jesus instructed His disciples exactly where to find a colt for Him to ride into Jerusalem, thereby fulfilling a prophecy revealed five hundred years earlier by Zechariah (Mark 11:1–11; Zechariah 9:9).

When you're organized and pay attention to detail, you'll be more productive, saving time and money. I cannot tell you how often I've wasted time looking for something that should have been returned to its rightful place. When I need to spend extra time searching for a file, my notes, or a resource, it's money lost that cannot be billed to a client. Time is *capital*!

Keeping workspaces physically clean and organized has multiple benefits, from protecting our stress levels and helping us focus to serving as a preventative law measure in keeping us out of litigation. Every CapitalMom needs the protection of a clean and organized workspace!

REGULARLY CLEANSING OUR HEARTS

We also need to consider spiritual cleanliness. Our spiritual lives mirror dirty laundry. The Bible says that "our righteous acts are like filthy rags..." (Isaiah 64:6 NIV). We are soiled daily, whether by telling a "small" lie, being easily angered by our children, failing to forgive others for their transgressions against us, or any other shortcoming.

So how do we regularly cleanse our hearts? We humble ourselves before God, seek His forgiveness, and repent. As Christians, we should regularly engage in repentance, or spiritual cleaning. We should pray, as David did: "Create in me a clean heart, O God; and renew a right spirit within me" (Psalm 51:10 KJV). By doing so, we are better prepared for the matters of parenting, business, and life we are sure to face.

EMBRACING THE POWER OF PRAYER

Shai and I begin every workday with a prayer. Normally we text it, but sometimes we send each other a voice message or pray in person. We seldom miss a day, but when it happens, we give ourselves grace and pick up where we left off.

When I recite the Lord's Prayer with my boys (Matthew 6:9–13; Luke 11:2–4) and we get to the words "forgive us our debts, as we forgive our debtors" (Matthew 6:12 KJV), I try to think of people I may be harboring unforgiveness and sins against, and to repent.

Starting your day off with a simple repentance prayer allows you to enjoy a fresh start spiritually. And spiritual cleanliness allows God's grace, mercy, and Spirit to work through you, building your gifts and establishing the framework for your business.

As you draw near to God, it shows forth through loving patience and kindness toward those around you, including your clients. When you feel spiritually clean, you are more peaceful and productive during your workday and at home. Everyone around us benefits when God cleanses our hearts.

GUARDING YOUR GIFT

As we have discussed before, God has gifted you with special talents, abilities, and passions that He wants you to grow and use. This gift is the foundation of your business. And because your gift is so valuable, it needs to be protected. God wants your gift to be honed and used in a maximum way so that it brings Him glory and serves others.

Too often, especially as a CapitalMom, we may be caught up in the busyness of life. Juggling many plates at the same time can distract us from doing the very thing that we were called to do. We also may not realize that when we don't protect our gifts legally, others may be able to undermine what we're doing.

Just as physical and spiritual cleanliness are necessary for us and our businesses to thrive, taking the steps needed to protect the gifts that God has given us will result in establishing fertile ground for growth.

MASTERING THE DELICATE
ART OF DELEGATION

As moms with an entrepreneurial spirit, we tend to pile our plates high until we get overwhelmed, but this isn't healthy. In fact, the more tasks we take on, the less we focus on our gifts—the talents, abilities, and passions that the Lord gave to us—and the more our businesses will suffer. Knowing all of this, I'm here to tell you that delegating is an integral part of being a CapitalMom.

An impressive example of delegation in Scripture is when Moses is advised by his father-in-law, Jethro, to delegate a substantial chunk of his cases to other judges (Exodus 18). At the time, Moses had been the only judge for matters concerning thousands of people. When Jethro realized how overwhelmed Moses had become and that he was creating a burden for himself and for his people, Jethro advised Moses to organize a team of judges for minor matters, while he remained the judge for the major cases. This delegation required Moses to take the time to teach others how to judge properly, but it would ultimately prove to be advantageous to Moses and to the people God led him to serve. I wonder how long Moses would have gone without help if Jethro hadn't given him that advice.

I imagine Moses had to pause his judgeship for a period to

train all of those new judges. Although delegating may initially feel burdensome and time consuming, it's necessary to ensure that you're the best version of yourself for your family and business. It's essential to recognize your need, and it's smart to delegate.

DELEGATING POORLY
VERSUS DELEGATING PROPERLY

Notice how Jethro advised Moses to delegate *and* to teach and instruct. Sometimes when we delegate, we assume that people will do things just as we do or provide the quality we require without giving them proper instructions. We need to understand that the instructions are equally as important as the delegation.

When I was in the Army, I delegated a job to a paralegal. I incorrectly assumed that the paralegal could manage the job without my instruction. When I requested an update on the job from the paralegal, I found out that it had not been completed and what had been done was not done correctly. I was extremely disappointed and ended up spending more time fixing the work that had been completed. My problem was not that I had delegated, but that I had not given the paralegal proper instruction.

On the other hand, one of the best business decisions Shai and I made together was to hire a bookkeeper early on in our business relationship. As a result, when the pandemic hit in 2020, it took only about an hour to accumulate the necessary documents and information to apply for the government's Payroll Protection Program. Because we didn't have to concern ourselves with bookkeeping, we freed up hours to use our gifts to help our clients, to attend to other business matters, and to spend with our families. Also, because we hired professionals in bookkeeping, we weren't required to be trained in bookkeeping.

No matter what you delegate as a small-business owner, it's important to be sure to have some idea of what that agent is doing on your behalf. For instance, the bookkeeper creates Profit and Loss (P & L) statements and files taxes for our business. Although we don't have a background in finance or accounting, our company is liable for the content of the tax forms that are sent to the government on our behalf. Therefore, it's imperative to understand exactly what you're delegating and to hire reputable companies as appropriate.

All entrepreneurs should seriously consider delegating tasks that make their business life easier and more successful. Here are more examples of common ways you can delegate in business:

- Hire your (age-appropriate) child to sweep, vacuum, and take out the trash at your office and at home. (Learn more about the tax benefits from a tax professional.)

- Hire a salesperson to score you big corporate gigs.

- Hire a marketing professional to post your social media ads.

- Hire a social media consultant to manage your company's social media accounts.

- Hire a grant writer to write your grant applications.

- Use a phone application to track your business mileage.

- Use a virtual assistant to answer your calls and schedule your appointments.

- Ask a friend to assist you with researching a few opportunities, nominate you for speaking gigs, and plan for the speaking opportunities by sticking labels on water bottles (or other marketing material) for you.

PROTECTING YOUR COMPANY (PLUS YOURSELF AND YOUR FAMILY) FROM LEGAL LIABILITY

As introduced in the December chapter, liability deals with the bottom line of who is legally responsible for something. This legal responsibility often equates to financial obligations but can require some other action, such as issuing an apology or amending your policies.

Sometime in 2021, I received a phone call from my middle child's teacher. She called to inform me that my son had hit another child in the eye region with a wooden block and the child was bleeding. She said that the class was frantic because the little boy gushed blood all over the floor. Everyone, including my son, was afraid. After being assured that the injured boy was okay, all I could think about was the legal liability we held if my son had caused the boy to go blind in one eye or if there were other medical expenses that would be due.

Just as a mother is responsible for the actions of her children, a business owner is liable for his or her business. However, the legal world created a way to protect business owners from being *personally* liable for the debts and liabilities of their companies. If you're personally liable, that may subject you (and your spouse) to monetary responsibility if your company is sued or owes a debt. Personal liability has caused some individuals to lose real estate (outside of their homestead) and cars in addition to their money. For example, in my story above, if the little boy's family were to accumulate $50,000 in medical bills because of my son's misconduct, my husband and I would be personally liable for those expenses. If we didn't have that amount in our bank account, a court could require us to sell our personal assets (outside of exempt property) to pay the debt!

In business, you can be personally liable for debts owed by the company, or you can form and register an actual business. By forming an actual company with your state, you can protect yourself from being personally liable for some debts and liabilities of your company. By forming a company, you are separating yourself from the company, making it a separate entity with its own liability.

When you have a part-time side hustle, you may not worry about being personally liable for the t-shirt that you screen print. You may only be required to reprint the shirt. But if you're baking goods or selling vehicles, you may want to have added protections just in case someone gets sick after eating a cupcake, or the vehicle someone purchased malfunctions, and there's suddenly a large lawsuit or debt connected to your business.

Keep in mind that when you first start a separate company, you may have a challenging time protecting yourself from certain liabilities, such as business credit. Lenders normally require the new business owner to sign as a guarantor of the credit. (The guarantor is responsible for paying in the event that a bill isn't paid by the original borrower.)

Here are a few ways to protect yourself from personal liability:

- Start a business entity with your state—for example, a limited liability company, a corporation, or a nonprofit.

- Sign a company agreement or bylaws.

- Adhere to your company agreement or bylaws.

- Open and use a separate bank account for the business.

- Keep meeting minutes, even if you're the only person in the "meeting."

- Maintain great record-keeping.

Don't take these steps for granted. Individuals have been found personally liable for their company's debts or liabilities when they've failed to operate the company as a separate entity.

THE BASICS OF PROACTIVELY PROTECTING YOUR INTELLECTUAL PROPERTY

Protecting your personal assets is extremely important, but it's equally important to protect your gifts and talents. You're a creative genius who deserves safeguarding.

If you have a unique name, a creative logo, or a revolutionary product, you may desire to protect it as your intellectual property. Protecting your intellectual property will allow you to have exclusive rights to the property so that no one may use it without your permission (which could be in the form of a license agreement and should result in passive income). There are four main types of intellectual property: copyright, trademarks, patents, and trade secrets.

Copyright: Who Owns What?

A copyright gives an owner the exclusive rights to original works of authorship. You may copyright artistic works, such as movies, songs, novels, poetry, blueprints, or software, or works of authorship, such as musicals, dramatics, or literary works. Copyrights expire after the life of the author plus seventy years. There are different expiration dates for anonymous works and works for hire. Copyrights are acquired through the U. S. Copyright Office.

A confusing fact is that we all have copyrights to our works without having to register them officially. However, to win a lawsuit more easily against someone for using your idea, you should have an official copyright. It also gives you leverage to negotiate license agreements with someone who wishes to use your material.

You may have heard of what's called the "poor man's copyright," which involves someone mailing a copy of their work to themselves and keeping it sealed. Although this may be evidence of when it was written, it doesn't create a formal copyright. For more information, visit www.copyright.gov.

Trademarks: The Little TM Symbols vs. the Circled ®s

A trademark (or a service mark) can be any symbol, name, word, device, or the combination thereof. The mark must be intended to identify the services or goods offered by a seller or provider and distinguish them from others. The mark indicates the *source* of the services or goods. Surnames, geographical locations, generic terms (and translations thereof), names and likenesses, and titles of books or movies cannot be trademarked.

A registered trademark is acquired through the United States Patent & Trademark Office (USPTO), but there are common law trademarks. You can simply add a small TM (or SM as appropriate) symbol to your mark to establish your intent to create a common law trademark. You don't have to register this mark or pay to do so. However, to have a registered trademark that protects your mark in all fifty states and fourteen territories of the United States, as well as the authority to use the circled "R," you must register your mark with the USPTO.

Keep in mind that to maintain registration with the USPTO, you must keep the trademark in commerce and file documentation in regular intervals (currently every ten years). Unlike patents and copyrights, trademark rights come from actual use and do not expire after a set term of years but require renewal. For more information, visit uspto.gov.

If you are not concerned about your mark's use across the country and territories but want to protect it in one state (for example, you may want to protect *Lone Star Salon* in Texas), you may register trademarks at the state level. It's normally a lot less expensive, and the application isn't as extensive. Visit your state's equivalent of the Secretary of State's office or website for more information.

Warning: only acquire a trademark when you're prepared financially, emotionally, and mentally to defend it. Otherwise, you could lose your trademark to someone else who is using it without opposition.

Patents: Protecting Your Inventions

Patents are property rights for inventions but may also be used to protect discoveries. Patents last between fifteen and twenty years, depending on the type of patent granted (design or utility, respectively). Processes, machines, manufacturers, compositions of matter, or "new and useful improvements" of them may be patented. You cannot patent a mere suggestion or idea. Most of the time, recipes don't qualify for patents, but those interested in patenting a recipe should speak with an experienced patent attorney for a legal opinion. Like trademarks, patents are acquired through the USPTO.

Trade Secrets: It Pays to Hush-Hush

Trade secrets are information that is unknown by the public and not readily available by legal means. You don't have to register a trade secret with a United States department or agency, but you must maintain secrecy (meaning disclosing it only on an as-needed basis) if you want to bring a successful trade secret cause of action.

Anytime I think of trade secrets, I think of Coca-Cola and my first time visiting their museum in Atlanta. If you haven't been, let me tell you that it's a spectacle. One thing the company makes clear during the visit is that their notorious refreshment's recipe is a trade secret. I would hate to be on the other end of a lawsuit brought by Coca-Cola for spilling the metaphorical beans.

In the event that you have a trade secret, such as a recipe or unique coding, you should at the very least have anyone and everyone who has access to the information sign a Confidentiality and/or Nondisclosure Agreement (NDA). This will make your attorney's life much easier if you must bring a lawsuit against someone for trade secret misappropriation.

As you can probably tell, there is overlap among the diverse types of intellectual property. If you're at all interested in protecting your intellectual property, consider delegating the task and consulting an attorney. Many attorneys offer free initial consultations and are happy to conduct an initial analysis for small-business owners.

Remember, in order to maintain intellectual property, you must protect it. If you allow a third party to use your product without a license and you don't litigate, you could expose yourself to losing rights to your own intellectual property!

It's Due Season!

Whoooh! You made it through this chapter!

After all that, we need a drink. A holy communion glass of wine.

My prayer is that after this chapter, you're able to grasp the importance of business cleanliness, organization, delegation, and protection. No one can do it for you, so make sure that you value and take the necessary steps for your business, your family, and yourself.

With that in mind, I invite you to repeat the following affirmations over your business for the next thirty days:

I value a clean workspace.

I value my myself, my customers, and my employees and, therefore, will maintain a clean workspace.

I value organization and delegation.

I value my time and others' time and, therefore, will be organized and will delegate.

I value assets.

I value my assets and the assets of others and will take the steps necessary to protect them.

April Notes

May:

Sow and Bloom Where You're Planted

Shinia Lambert

Do good, and care not to whom.[33] —**Italian Proverb**

Plant [verb]: to put or set in the ground for growth.[34]

You've sown the seed of entrepreneurship by starting a business that you feel called to, gifted for, and passionate about. In this season, you're ready to bloom and see your business take off. But there's something else about this season that's special: it's time to share your gift with others.

To bloom and truly become who God created you to be involves serving others—and it's one of the most important and special aspects of this season. It begins by asking, "How may I help you?" And it expands into a wholehearted commitment to your growth, as well as that of your business and those you are called to serve. That may look different for each of us practically, but biblically it comes down to two foundational and scriptural commands: love God and love others. (If you need a refresher on what love looks like for yourself and your business, revisit our February chapter).

OUR RELATIONSHIP WITH GOD IMPACTS OUR RELATIONSHIP WITH OTHERS

Let's face it: as CapitalMoms, we have full plates. But having full plates doesn't have to translate into feeling overwhelmed or putting ourselves in a position that jeopardizes our mental health. If there is one foundational truth, one piece of advice, one smidgen of wisdom that I can give you, it would be this: don't forget to love yourself. This isn't merely a suggestion. God desires it. I would be so bold as to say that He commands it. He wants us to love Him, love others, and love ourselves.

Mark 12:30–31 reads, "'Love the Lord your God with all your heart and with all your soul and with all your mind and with all your strength.' The second is this: 'Love your neighbor as yourself.' There is no commandment greater than these" (NIV).

God wants us to understand that a healthy vertical relationship with Him requires and will produce a healthy horizontal relationship with others. But there is something hidden in verse 31 that I don't think we talk about enough.

It's that little part at the end that says, "...as yourself."

We're called to love our neighbors as we love ourselves. That implies that we must first love ourselves. If we don't, by which standard are we to love our neighbors? If we have not yet begun to acknowledge the uniqueness and beauty that we possess, how can we see the image of God in others? How can we esteem our neighbors while devaluing ourselves? I can't. Can you? In other words, a healthy relationship with God produces a healthy view of ourselves, and out of the love we have for God and for ourselves, we can love others.

SELF-LOVE DOES NOT EQUAL SELFISHNESS!

Are you uncomfortable right now? Is this preposterous idea that you are expected to love yourself making you squirm? Can I tell you why this makes you so uncomfortable? Because you're used to putting your energy and love into others, so the very mention of loving yourself brings feelings of guilt. If this is you, we are going to settle this matter right now—not just because it hinders your service (and it does), but because you are worthy of resolving this issue of self-love. Self-love does not equal selfishness. It's not about a spa day, a vacation, or a trip to Target, even though I love all those things.

Self-love means being okay with being in the present, acknowledging that you are enough (without having to qualify that statement), forgiving yourself for the things you didn't know, believing that you are who God says you are, giving yourself grace to make mistakes, accepting yourself the way you are right now (flaws and all), being okay with uncertainty, and freeing yourself to take risks. That, my friend, is what it means to love yourself! It is affording yourself the same grace you so freely give to others. It's being kind to yourself. It's allowing yourself to feel an emotion without apologizing for it. It's asking for help and not feeling guilty. It's setting boundaries and enforcing them. That is loving yourself, and that's a good thing.

You are the basis of your business. If you don't love yourself, you won't value the gift(s) God gave you or what you bring to your business. And if you can deny the uniqueness that you bring to the table, you will undercut and undervalue your business. When you diminish the value of your business, you diminish your ability to serve others. How? You are not likely to promote a business you don't believe has anything significant or worthy to offer. You're not going to network and articulate to others how you can meet their needs if you're not confident that you can. You won't seek to be the answer to anyone's prayer or the solution to anyone's problem if you don't think that you possess any value. This is something we all must get right!

We have something that the marketplace needs. We have no business (no pun intended!) withholding the gift we possess or using it only for ourselves. The Lord gave us the gift to share with others, whether it's in the form of our services, goods, or programs. People deserve what we have, and it is within our power to give it to them. This is how we successfully love our neighbors in the marketplace, and it begins with seeing ourselves clearly and understanding the value we possess.

SERVING OTHERS WITHOUT LOVE

I love the way 1 Corinthians 13:1–3 reads: "If I speak with human eloquence and angelic ecstasy but don't love, I'm nothing but the creaking of a rusty gate. If I speak God's Word with power, revealing all his mysteries and making everything plain as day, and if I have faith that says to a mountain, 'Jump,' and it jumps, but I don't love, I'm nothing. If I give everything I own to the poor and even go to the stake to be burned as a martyr, but I don't love, I've gotten nowhere. So, no matter what I say, what I believe, and what I do, I'm bankrupt without love" (MSG).

Our acts of service are meaningless—they are nothing—if they are not done in love! There is no such thing as checking people off like tasks on your to-do list. People require relationship.

Relationship doesn't always mean reciprocity. Being in relationship doesn't always mean that we'll be appreciated. But relationship does mean service, and serving God's way cannot be done without love for God, love for ourselves, and love for the people we are serving.

THE HEART OF A SUCCESSFUL BUSINESS

At the heart of a successful business is service. What do you have that other people need? We touched on this in the January chapter when we helped you to identify and clearly articulate your "why," your exciting proposition, and your contribution to the world.

Another way to articulate this is to ask yourself, "What problem have I been created to solve?" or "What is an issue that frustrates me enough to take action?" The answer to these questions is your call to serve, and you can serve and make a profit at the same time. I know, *gasp*! As both business owners and believers, we desire for you to understand that God is not anti-entrepreneur, He is not anti-profit, He is not anti-wealth, and He is not anti-living your best life.

In a conversation we had with a staff member who helped us to publish this book, he shared that he has seen in the church a teaching trend that masks scarcity as good stewardship. Wow, I cannot deny the truth in that statement. We must let go of the idea that service and stewardship mean that we must live lives of scarcity. Scarcity is not, in and of itself, a good or terrible thing. God looks upon the heart and honors good stewardship, whether you have a little or a lot.

We have found that if we prove to be good stewards, the more God blesses us with, the more we get to pour out. That has been a critical part of our vision as CapitalMoms. We prayed for an influx of income, not so we could flaunt our finances, but so we could pour into others, without hesitation and with God's leading, to help meet their needs and see other entrepreneurs' dreams come true.

Your vision doesn't have to mimic ours. What we want you to take away from this is the idea that it's okay to be financially successful, but that's not our end goal. We don't desire to be wealthy for wealth's sake. We acknowledge that God is the source of every resource, that all things belong to Him, and we want to honor Him with our success, including financially. When we rid ourselves of the scarcity mindset, we stop putting God in a box and realize that His resources are endless.

We can ask for more because we are willing to give more. We can pour out more because we believe that God will provide and equip us with all we need. As our desires begin to align with His desires, we get to partner with Him to bring His kingdom agenda into fruition and see real transformation in the communities and clients we serve. It all begins with a heart of service, of which no greater example can be found than the attitude and life of Christ.

A SPIRIT OF SERVANTHOOD

A spirit of servanthood requires that we consider the needs of others while not neglecting our own. It also recognizes the value in others while refusing to pursue selfish ends or get big heads. Philippians 2:3–5 reads, "Do nothing out of selfish ambition or conceit, but in humility consider others as more important than yourselves. Everyone should look not to his own interests, but rather to the interests of others. Adopt the same attitude as that of Christ Jesus" (CSB).

Christ was God in the flesh, but He was also a servant. There is no greater name proclaimed through all the earth, no man who has left a greater impact on the planet, yet He was a servant. This approach to success—the idea that you can be humble, seek others' interests above your own, and still win—is counterintuitive to the prevailing culture. Servanthood takes spiritual maturity.

Dr. Tony Evans states, "Love is a choice to serve someone for his or her good. It is a decision of the will, which is why we can, and should, love people even if we don't like them." [35]

Did you notice that? Service has nothing to do with liking people; it's about loving them. In your business and in this world, you will serve people who look different from you, act differently from you, and have beliefs that are different from yours. You are called to serve them anyway. I will say it again: it's not about liking people (although if not liking people has anything to do with what they believe or how they look, then we need to spend some time together in the July chapter very soon); it's about loving them.

So, what does it mean to love someone? In his book *Relational Intelligence*, Dr. Dharius Daniels explains, "We've bought the lie that we are supposed to feel the same way about everybody. But biblically this isn't even true. There are several ways to love that show up in the Bible. And the one often talked about—agape, a Greek word—has nothing to do with feelings at all. It's a love of the will. It's an unconquerable benevolence. It's commitment to do what's in the best interest of someone else, regardless of what they do for you." [36]

Now, hear me clearly. I am not trying to perpetuate this idea of scarcity again, that we should give our services away for free because we are called to love and serve or that making a profit with a successful business is counter-Christian. I'm saying that if God has burdened your heart with a need or a passion so great that you are committed to sowing in that area, you don't have to know exactly how you will reap! Sit with that for a minute.

Through personal experience and the testimony of others, I have found that the trajectory from the business concept to the manifestation of what we would call success is rarely a straight line. What felt like a burden in one season was appreciated as a blessing in another. What seemed like a tedious and grueling grind in one season felt like a training session in another. The thread of consistency that connected all the seasons, however, was the heart of service, the underlying "why."

It's important to understand that service is twofold: (1) your "why," which is the crux of your business and how you specifically meet the needs of your niche and customer base, and (2) how your business can serve the community and be socially responsible.

CORPORATE SOCIAL RESPONSIBILITY: FROM GLOBAL TO LOCAL

Corporate social responsibility (CSR) is a model that helps a company to be socially accountable to itself, its employees, its shareholders, and the public. Companies that have CSR programs or various CSR-related activities, such as philanthropy and volunteer efforts, can be conscious of the social, economic, and environmental impact they are having on society. While one obvious benefit of CSR is that it helps society, it can also help a company's brand.[37]

Here are two inspiring examples that illustrate what CSR looks like.

Lego's Commitment to Sustainability

Since 2014, Lego has been part of the World Wildlife Fund's Climate Savers program and has pledged to reduce its carbon impact. In coming years, the toymaker plans to use environmentally friendly materials to produce all of its core products and packaging.[38]

To achieve that goal, the toymaker is investing $164 million into its Sustainable Materials Center, where researchers are experimenting with bio-based materials that can be implemented into the production process.[39]

Starbucks's Commitment to Ethical Sourcing

In 2002, Starbucks launched its first CSR report with the goal of committing to ethical sourcing. In 2015, Starbucks verified that, via partnerships with local coffee farmers and organizations, 99 percent of its coffee supply chain was ethically sourced. But even that wasn't good enough for the global coffee brand. Indeed, in the future, Starbucks plans to source 100 percent of its supply chain ethically. [40] For its work, Starbucks was named one of the world's most ethical companies in 2021.[41]

Yes, Lego and Starbucks are large corporations, but the inspiration we can glean from these examples is that there are tangible ways our businesses can contribute to and serve our local communities, and these contributions matter!

Here are some ways you can get involved locally while also marketing and branding your business:

- Join local Chambers of Commerce and get involved with workshops and networking. Most chambers host events that spotlight small businesses who also give back to the community. Volunteer to host a meeting if you have a brick-and-mortar, or sponsor refreshments if you don't.

- Host a food or toy drive during the holiday season. This can be as simple as letting your business location be the drop-off spot for goods and agreeing to transport them to the local food bank or shelter.

- Volunteer to clean up the community garden in your branded T-shirt. (Don't be afraid to get your hands dirty!)

- Run a 5K for a charity you believe in while wearing your branded T-shirt.

- Pass out water with your company's name on the bottles to people in voter registration or election lines.

- Partner with other businesses to provide discounted or free services to families or individuals in need. Don't forget your business card because word of mouth is still the best marketing.

- Offer free consultations or workshops or be a guest speaker at events in exchange for an opportunity to promote your services. Be ready to hand out a brochure, pamphlet, or flier detailing your services and have a sign-up sheet ready for those who may want to follow up with you.

CSR IS GOOD FOR BUSINESSES AND YOUR SOUL

There are many things you can do to get involved in your community. People tend to think that serving or volunteering are opportunities reserved for non-profit organizations, yet small for-profit businesses are often a force for good in their communities, serving, giving back, and partnering with other businesses and organizations.

Another myth that needs to be addressed is the concept that for-profit businesses are giving back only when they use their profits to serve a need in the local or global community. When we promote the idea that for-profit businesses give back only when they donate a portion of their profits to charities, we are simultaneously promoting the thought that the for-profit businesses do not have any inherent value, that they are not in themselves doing good and serving their communities. This could not be further from the truth!

Businesses serve their communities by selling. Because that business exists, there is a good, a service, or a program that the consumer needs. In fact, there is a consumer need met by every business, and that fact alone makes a business inherently valuable to the community it serves, whether locally or globally. It's important for us to understand this because it shapes how we view our businesses and the value we attach to them.

Rabbi Daniel Lapin digs deeper into this mindset in *Thou Shall Prosper: Ten Commandments for Making Money*.[42] In this book, Lapin reminds us that we must view our for-profit businesses as "moral."

Your business is a worthy cause. It's providing quality services or goods that people need, and they compensate you with "certificates of appreciation" that we call money. There is no shame in that. We must rid ourselves of a scarcity mindset that pervades the Christian community and makes us believe that to succeed and do well financially, or to *want* to succeed and do well financially, is sinful, immoral, or selfish. Our businesses can be both "this" and "that." We can make a significant profit while also adding value to the community.

On the other hand, you may have a heart and mission specifically for starting a non-profit organization to serve your community. For example, my son Aidan has a heart for serving the homeless, so we started Maddox Ministries, Inc., in 2020 to provide food and other necessities seasonally to our local homeless population.

Many components of forming a for-profit business and a non-profit business are the same, yet non-profits do possess some unique characteristics worth mentioning. The next section will give you an idea of what you need to do if you feel led to start a non-profit and serve your community in this way.

How to Start a Non-Profit

When it comes to forming a business, non-profit or otherwise, it can be done on your own. However, it's not the best practice if you don't have the time to invest in doing it properly. As far as paperwork goes, forming a non-profit isn't much different from forming any other type of company. In fact, you'll likely find that your state charges far less to form and register a non-profit business than it does for other business entities. But there a couple things you want to be aware of, such as specific language that your state may require to be included in your formation documents or bylaws, and who or what is required to form a proper Board of Directors.

Because the term "Board of Directors" sounds intimidating, forming one can seem equally daunting. But it doesn't have to be that way. It's important to know that all non-profits are required to have a Board of Directors. The responsibilities of each board member may vary depending on the organization's mission, but all boards generally have a threefold purpose: legal, ethical, and practical. Boards maintain the culture of the non-profit and preserve the checks and balances of the organization. How your board members operate will be detailed in your bylaws.

Ebony and I are huge proponents of entrepreneurs joining

boards of local non-profit and professional organizations, and we both serve diligently on one or more. The best way to understand how a board works is to immerse yourself into one. This is another great way to consider giving back to and serving your community while also reaping the benefits of hands-on experience and networking opportunities.

Most non-profits, once properly formed, will request tax-exempt status from the federal government via the Internal Revenue Service. First, determine if your organization meets the eligibility requirements, which vary depending on the nature of your non-profit and its mission. Second, gather your organization's formation documents. You'll need to reference them during the application process and may also need to include them with your application. Third, you want to determine your state's registration requirements regarding formation and bylaws.

The most common type of tax-exempt status is the 501(c)(3) status, which we will cover below. When it comes to filing documents with the IRS, we highly recommend that you work with a tax professional and/or an attorney who handles non-profit law and is familiar with these forms. You'll want to stay away from websites that pretend to be associated with the IRS and offer products for payment that either don't accomplish what you're after or offer little to no assistance regarding what to do next.

We certainly do not pretend to be all-knowing when it comes to the IRS and filing taxes. That's why we hire tax professionals for ourselves and our business. However, when it comes to non-profits and obtaining your 501(c)(3) status, we have learned a thing or two about which forms to file and when. We hope that this basic outline of information can help you to make a decision regarding how to proceed.

501(c)(3) Status

To qualify for 501(c)(3) status, an organization must be established for one of the following reasons:

- Religious

- Charitable

- Scientific

- Testing for public safety

- Literary

- Educational

- Other specified purposes that meet certain other requirements[43]

What are the benefits of 501(c)(3) status?

- Exemption from taxes

- Seems more credible

- Gives donors tax deductions

- Eligibility for grants on federal, state, and local levels

- Discounted postage rates

- Discounts on marketing

Be mindful that while there are benefits, there are also restrictions in place that you must adhere to in order to maintain your 501(c)(3) status.

Which Form Is Right for You?

From my experience, one of the main reasons why entrepreneurs are hesitant to tackle tax-exempt status is the application process. The IRS is known for making things, well, as clear as mud, to say the least. However, with the right information and assistance, tax-exempt status can be yours.

To begin, the IRS requires that you apply online via one of two forms: the 1023 EZ or the 1023 form. With the 1023 EZ form, think of "EZ" as meaning "easy." Why? Because the former is the shorter form by far, totaling about three pages, while the original 1023 form is closer to thirty! The EZ form has seventeen prerequisites, but there are three standout questions that will help you to determine whether it's the appropriate form for you:

1. Do you anticipate that your non-profit's annual gross receipts will exceed $50,000 in any of the following three years after the application is filed, or have the receipts exceeded $50,000 in the three years prior to filing the application?

2. Do the total assets of your non-profit, at fair market value, exceed $250,000?

3. Are you forming a church?

If your answer is "yes" to any of these questions, then you cannot file the 1023 EZ, and your only option is to use the original 1023. Do not despair! While the 1023 is long and requires extensive financial information, no one has better access to that information than you. As far as it taking more time, most good things do. This is also a great opportunity for you to delegate! Consider hiring a tax professional, whether it be a bookkeeper, CPA, or attorney, to assist you with your application.

IT'S DUE SEASON!

Remember: a healthy relationship with God produces a healthy relationship with yourself. Out of the love you have for God and for yourself, you can better love and serve others. Spend some time this month reflecting on how well you are loving yourself. Use these journaling prompts to get you started:

- Am I self-aware? Do I know the kind of person I am and the kind of person I want to become?

- Am I holding on to any limiting beliefs that keep me from fully loving myself while also acknowledging areas in which I need to grow?

- Am I able to identify five things that I love about myself?

- Am I taking time daily to invest in myself? Am I edifying, educating, and empowering myself?

- Am I at peace with God, and have I fully accepted His unconditional love for me?

May Notes

PART THREE: SUMMER

June:
Walking on Beach Water

Ebony Todd

Take a leap of faith and see that these troubled waters
have no power over you unless you give it to them, and
even then they lie.[44]

—Ted Dekker, *Water Walker*

Faith [verb]: trust, confidence, and hope.

I adore the title of this chapter. When I came up with it, I
wanted to pat myself on the back! I can't help but associate
walking on water with the story of Peter getting out of a boat
and walking to Jesus on the water. I'll give you an Ebony version of the story found in Matthew 14:22–33.

Jesus had just sent His disciples away by boat to
Gennesaret, where He would meet up with them, heal more
sick people, and teach more arrogant Pharisees (I'm not just
being critical; that's biblical). After sending His disciples on

ahead of Him, Jesus stayed behind in Nazareth to say good-bye to His people and find a quiet place to pray.

Meanwhile, as the disciples made their way to Gennesaret on the boat, a storm brewed on the sea and tossed the boat around as the waves towered above them. I imagine that they were all hugging each other. Or maybe they were trying to act all manly while looking at each other, not wanting to be the first one to cry. Anyway, at "ol' dark thirty" (which translates biblically to something like 3 o'clock in the morning), Jesus approached the boat in the middle of the sea. He was literally walking to the boat on the water.

Now the men on the boat wet their pants (it's my version of the story, so don't judge) and cry out because they thought that Jesus was a ghost! Jesus reminded them that it was Him, which you would think the disciples would have figured out since He had on the same outfit from just a few hours ago. But the disciples were still not convinced. Peter decided that he would be the toughest of them all and triple dog dare Jesus by saying, in so many words, "If You are the Lord, then allow me to walk to You on the water."

Jesus was like, "Don't threaten Me with a good time. Walk to Me!" Peter walked out on the water to Jesus, but when the storm picked up again, Peter shook in fear and began to sink. As you can imagine, Peter began to whimper like a puppy.

Jesus said, "Wow, look at how little faith you have! Why did you ever think that I would let you drown?" In a split second, Jesus rescued Peter from drowning.

Do you want me to translate the entire Bible? DM me if you do!

This story is commonly used by pastors and preachers to teach the importance of faith. Later in the Gospel of Matthew, Jesus told His disciples that if they had "faith as small as a mustard seed," they would be empowered to move mountains (Matthew 17:20). What amazes me is that, in my mind, the disciples (especially Peter) had faith of extreme magnitude. Besides the fact that they all left their loved ones and careers to follow and learn from Jesus, Peter took it one step further and got out of the boat onto turbulent water to walk toward Jesus. Is this not faith, Lord? But to Jesus, even doing that didn't fully demonstrate Peter's faith!

YOUR WILLINGNESS TO STEP OUT IN FAITH IS AN ASSET TO BEING AN ENTREPRENEUR

Like in Peter's story, your level of faith can determine whether you sink or excel as an entrepreneur. When I think of entrepreneurial faith, I think of my business partner, Shai. I started the law office alone, as a mom with two kids, but my Army Officer husband sustained our household and supported my business venture. Although I naturally met challenges, I didn't feel that my faith was being tested in that moment.

But when I met Shai, the mud was removed from my eyes, and I was blessed to witness entrepreneurial faith. Shai was a single mother of a kindergartener, with a mortgage (amongst other bills) and a job with the state of Texas that provided her with a healthy salary and great benefits.

151

I feel odd comparing myself to Jesus, but I believe that you'll catch the message I'm about to relay. In the moment when I asked Shai to join me as partner at the law firm, she probably felt like one of the disciples, perhaps most like Peter. Maybe she felt like I was telling her to get out of the boat and put her big toe in the water. But she did it. She did it with grace and without flinching because of what I believe to be her faith not only in me and herself, but most of all, in God.

Little did we know that within six months of our partnership in the law firm, a pandemic would hit the entire world. When the pandemic initially hit, I often wondered if she regretted leaving her valuable salary and superb benefits. Each time I would inquire, Shai reassured me that she never once regretted making the decision to join me in the water. Although we've had months when we didn't make our goal income, we've never missed a rent payment. We were able to take home a check every month, despite the decrease in clients at the height of the pandemic. Oddly enough, there were months when we exceeded our goals and made more money than we made before the pandemic.

The fact that we hung in there and even prospered at times during the pandemic goes against the statistics. The Federal Reserve Bank of New York released a brief naming Black businesses as more than twice as likely to close as a result of the pandemic. Between February and April 2020, the number of active Black businesses fell 41 percent while the number of white businesses fell by 17 percent.[45] Moreover, a study of North American businesses at the start of the pandemic found that 17 percent of male-owned businesses had closed compared to 30 percent of female-owned businesses.[46]

Our business, being Black- and female-owned, had low odds of surviving the pandemic. Had we wavered and taken our eyes off our purpose and promise, we might have sunk. I believe that it was our faith that brought us through and managed to increase our income after a year of the coronavirus.

We've also had the pleasure of serving as general counsel for a client who left a well-paying job to start her own business in the middle of the pandemic. Talk about faith! Norman Vincent Peale, minister and author of *The Power of Positive Thinking*, wrote back in the 1950s, "Believe in yourself! Have faith in your abilities! Without a humble but reasonable confidence in your own powers you cannot be successful or happy." [47] I must agree that after faith in God, having faith in yourself will enable your success.

HOW TO USE "S. A. N. D."
TO SHOW YOUR FAITH

Whether people are believers or not, it takes faith to start a business, but many may not realize the amount of faith it takes to *rest* as an entrepreneur. In fact, I consider it one of the hardest tasks for me to complete!

Lori Greiner, entrepreneur, inventor, and star of ABC's *Shark Tank*, has been credited with saying, "Entrepreneurs are the only people who will work 80 hours a week to avoid working 40 hours a week." [48] There's so much truth to that statement!

I gladly work harder for myself and my business partner than for anyone else. The problem is that, being a wife and a mother of three, having a career, having two businesses while starting a third, serving on boards and as an associate municipal court judge, chair for one organization, vice-chair for another, and committee chair for a group, and volunteering for yet more, all while authoring my first book, I have a hard time exercising the faith it takes to rest. Still, when I'm "walking on beach water," I love the S. A. N. D.

S. A. N. D. = Sleep + Abandon + Nurture + Disconnect

Sleep

New parents lose sleep at least the first year of their babies' lives. Did you know that sleep deprivation after giving birth has been shown to accelerate your aging?[49] Similar to having a new baby, when you have a new business, you likely go to sleep and wake up thinking of it. It may not wake you up in the middle of the night, but if you're not getting enough sleep, you must prioritize rest. Otherwise, you may grow too biologically old and tired to finish the race!

Abandon

It's imperative that in the S. A. N. D., you practice self-control and *do not work*. You may be thinking, *"Easier said than done."* But I petition you to do the hard thing, take the bull by its horns, and don't check your email! Don't work on the project! Don't study! And while you're at it, live on the edge, be a little reckless, and don't answer the call! Refrain from labor while you're in the S. A. N. D.

Nurture

Take care of yourself!
You might have heard or used this old adage as a parting statement. Raise your hand if you *actually* part ways with the person who has challenged you (in fact, ordered you) to nurture yourself and oblige them by speaking positive affirmations in the mirror, eating a healthy meal, having a spa day, and ridding yourself of all negative relationships.

Hand still down? I thought so.

While in the S. A. N. D., do all of that.

Disconnect

I don't think we need to take a long time to understand the value of this final aspect of S. A. N. D. Raise your hand if you long for disconnection from social media, the internet, the phone, the email, the clients and customers, the children, and all other responsibilities.

Raising both hands? I thought so.

While in the S. A. N. D., do that, too.

START MAKING YOUR S. A. N. D. CASTLE

It takes great faith to stop working on your business, especially as a small-business owner. In the United States, there are millions of small businesses that have only one employee—the owner. According to Chamberof Commerce.org, there are 22 million individually operated small businesses in the U. S.![50]

When I was the only person working in my office, I didn't even consider taking days off. In fact, on my very first day of operation, I was sitting in front of my first paying client when I received a phone call from the daycare to pick up my one-year-old, who had come down with a fever. I didn't hesitate—I towed him to work with me until at least twenty-four hours after he was "fever-free without fever-reducing medications."

There was no way I could lock my doors for twenty-four hours (absent a weekend) when I had just opened my business. Though I'm grateful for the success of my career up to this point, I also know that if this were to happen again, I would schedule some S. A. N. D. time after my son was well again.

You may notice that Shai and I cover self-care topics quite frequently in this book. We do so because it's a subject that professional women often struggle with. Time and again, we see the lack of self-care and taking time off with women entrepreneurs and career women in general. I'm so invested in the mission of promoting self-care among professional women that I created a business with a couple of my close friends centered around edifying the professional woman and her self-care journey. (If you'd like more information on how you can practice self-care as a professional woman and/or want support in your journey, visit www.WeCover-Down.com.)

S. A. N. D. doesn't have to be long, and it shouldn't be stressful. If you spend the entire time thinking of work, then you've defeated the purpose. This is not an opportunity to brainstorm business ideas or solutions to your clients' problems. Instead, trust that your work will be there when you return. Your customers will honor and respect your need for time off. Your children will be blessed to have a more refreshed mother. Your family will support your endeavor to care for yourself. And most importantly, your God will never fail you (1 Corinthians 1:9; 1 Chronicles 28:20).

For me, the following passage captures these sentiments perfectly:

> *Remember the Sabbath day, to keep it holy. Six days you shall labor, and do all your work, but the seventh day is a Sabbath to the LORD your God. On it you shall not do any work, you, or your son, or your daughter, your male servant, or your female servant, or your livestock, or the sojourner who is within your gates. For in six days the LORD made heaven and earth, the sea, and all that is in them, and rested on the seventh day. Therefore the LORD blessed the Sabbath day and made it holy.*
> *—Exodus 20:8–11 (ESV)*

Although I believe that Jesus died for our sins and

loosened us from the bondage of the many traditions and practices of the Old Testament, I also believe that the principles of the Old Testament ring true. If God *required* rest, why would I trust myself *without* it?

In fact, rest is of so much importance that it is referred to almost three hundred times in the Bible. Rest is not only a biblical principle, but a scientific one as well. Studies show that our immune systems fail us when we don't allow our bodies ample time to rest. Furthermore, without rest, our minds are unable to perform optimally. According to author and entrepreneur Rhett Power, there are twelve reasons to give yourself a day of rest as proclaimed in the book of Exodus.[51] Time away from work:

1. Reduces stress

2. Gives you more time to move

3. Reduces inflammation and risk of heart disease

4. Boosts your immune system

5. Reduces sleep-disrupting habits

6. Adds years to your life

7. Restores mental energy

8. Enables creativity

9. Enables productivity

10. Improves focus at work

11. Improves short-term memory

12. Helps you to enjoy work more

Some Fortune 500 companies have accepted the benefits of rest, so much so that they've implemented ways to ensure that their employees rest. As stated by Mr. Powers, their efforts have proven that rest maximizes creativity, productivity, and memory. It also increases morale and promotes retention. Companies like Facebook, Google, and Ben & Jerry's have designated areas for their employees to nap. This may seem unreasonable for some, especially for entrepreneurs who are just starting out, but taking a twenty-minute nap twice a week has proven to improve the quality of life and work.

One way Shai and I have ensured that we have time to rest and time to work is to designate days of meeting with clients and prospective clients. We meet with clients three days of the week. This leaves the other two days of the week for us to work without interruption, ensuring that we'll have time for rest as well. Since implementing this plan, I feel much better about my work product and am less stressed throughout the week. I don't stress about finding time to complete a task, because I generally get my work done on one of the two days we've designated. I also try to complete other tasks that must be done, such as visiting my sons' schools or going to the post office, during work hours.

But what about resting for one full day every week?

Give "Sabbathing" a Chance

As a mother, I often find it hard to commit to taking a full day off to rest. There isn't a day of the week when I feel like I have truly not labored, but I guess that depends on how we define *labor*. I find it laborious to referee fights between my two boys, cook, do laundry, help with homework, prepare for the week ahead, and clean up. And believe it or not, these are most of the tasks that I do on my Sabbath. "Sabbathing" is tough to do as a mother, but we should still do it!

Priscilla Shirer has an entire Bible study and book dedicated to teaching women to observe a Sabbath. It's called *Breathe: Making Room for Sabbath.*[52] As I listened to her preach to my soul, I felt like I had been failing myself, my family, and my future by not honoring a day of rest.

Your Sabbath does not have to be on the weekend. Once I wrapped my mind around that fact, I felt enlightened and empowered to give "Sabbathing" a chance. Sometimes my Sabbath changes. Some weeks I must give myself grace when I forget to have a Sabbath or simply refuse to have one. As a CapitalMom, it's difficult to observe a Sabbath. Between our children and our business, things are required of us daily.

Even as I am writing this very paragraph at 4 a.m. on a Saturday (my daughter woke me at 3:30 a.m. to eat), I'm pumping milk for Monday. I don't find this activity at all "Sabbathy." And when I wake up and frantically get everyone ready for church on Sunday, I don't feel "Sabbathy." However, there are times during the week after I've dropped the kids off at school and daycare that I find my Sabbath. It's a time to sit, read the Word, pray, and feel less pressure to get anything done.

Resting is as much a part of life as breathing for all living organisms. When you plan out your week, try including mandatory rest. What rest looks like for each of us varies. Remember that rest requires a certain level of faith for any entrepreneur, but especially for a CapitalMom balancing business and motherhood. Respect the role that rest has in your life by prioritizing it to the benefit of yourself, your family, and your future. Regardless of *when* we take our Sabbath, we all should take the leap of faith needed to rest one day a week.

EFFECTIVE DELEGATION REQUIRES FAITH

Do you know that it takes faith to delegate responsibilities and hire employees or independent contractors? You may be thinking, *"I've read about delegation. Enough already!"* But there's another great point I wish to make about delegation and faith.

Trusting that someone will get a job done to your standards and when you want it done is often a challenge. There were many times when I failed to delegate while leading an organization because I didn't trust anyone else to do the job or I was uncomfortable asking for help. This not only caused me grief, but was often to the detriment of the entire organization. When I tried to do everything myself, the organization accomplished less and my work product suffered.

These days, I ain't got that issue! I'm quick to identify other people's gifts and talents, ask for assistance, and graciously thank the people who help me along the way. As revealed in an earlier chapter, I may give a little too much freedom to the people I'm delegating to, so I must backtrack to ensure that I have given them enough instruction and guidance to pull the task off. Nonetheless, when it comes to entrepreneurship, it is of dire importance that when you're ready to delegate tasks more permanently (i.e., hire independent contractors and/or employees), you understand the implications of and generally know the laws that govern agency, hiring, and firing.

AGENTS, PRINCIPALS, EMPLOYEES, CONTRACTORS—WHO IS WHO?

Under state and federal agency laws, you may be held personally responsible for the acts and contracts entered into by an *agent*. Agents are entrusted to conduct matters on behalf of their *principal*, which, in your case, would be you. Agency relationships are generally of consensual creation, and no written agreement is required. Agency relationships are not limited to actual employment. They are created when we send our sons into restaurants to purchase food for the family and when we have our neighbors pick up our daughters from school with their daughters.

However, agency relationships are only enforceable when they're created for legal purposes. For instance, it is illegal for a therapist to employ unlicensed agents to perform a therapist's job that requires licensure. Therefore, the agency relationship and any contract of the illegal nature between the two parties would be unenforceable in court.

Many times, business owners employ employees and independent contractors to be their agents. Knowing the difference between the two is imperative for federal and state tax purposes.

Determining whether a worker is an employee or an independent contractor depends on several factors and has been a point of contention in court cases and IRS audits. Generally, employees are workers who are *controlled* by their employers, who are responsible for determining the details of their employees' work. The employer directs and/or supervises the employee's work and provides the employee with the supplies and tools necessary to perform the job. There are other factors that may be considered, but these are some of the weightiest.

Independent contractors, on the other hand, have more control over their work and schedule than employees do. They may be hired by an employer, but that employer typically doesn't provide the supplies or tools needed to provide the service. Moreover, the employer doesn't supervise or direct the independent contractor's work. Some examples are when you hire an accountant, plumber, or painter who has his or her own company.

Please note: these definitions are generic, and there are exceptions to almost every rule in the legal world. But defining

whether someone you pay to work is an employee or an independent contractor is important because it determines:

1. Whether you report that person as an employee to the state and the IRS

2. Whether you issue a W-2 or a 1099 (these are IRS documents) to that individual or company

3. Whether you must pay payroll taxes

Additionally, depending on your state and profession, you may be required to carry workman's compensation and/or insurance for yourself and your employees. Hiring employees can be costly, and making the leap to adding employees should be well thought out and budgeted.

THE POWER OF CLEAR EXPECTATIONS

In the event that you decide your business is ready to hire an employee, it is imperative that expectations are managed for all parties involved. You can manage expectations with your employee handbook, training, and (for some) an employment contract. Managing expectations is a preventative measure to deter unnecessary and costly unemployment claims.

Employee Handbook

When writing your company policies, don't simply copy and paste generic pre-written policies from somewhere else. Instead, you should write them so that they give you and your employees an idea of your personal expectations and acceptable practices in your industry. You should have policies that cover leave, the process to report tardiness, payroll, ways to handle disputes, and many other subjects.

Keep in mind that there are some policies that cannot be put in place because they are against the law, and some policies require express consent. For example, in Texas, you can't condition an employee's employment based on non-membership in a union. It's also illegal to terminate or impose an adverse job action on an employee in retaliation for an employee refusing to commit a criminal offense.

If you need assistance with an employee handbook, you can use online resources, hire an attorney, or contact your state's government agency that assists employers.

No matter what your policies are, it's important that you abide by them. That's the only way they will be useful for unemployment claim purposes. From a legal advocacy standpoint, if you have policies but fail to follow them, you may as well not have the policies at all!

Training

Training is necessary and invaluable. It empowers your employees to feel confident that they are capable and prepared to do the job and can prevent some disruption and distractions down the road. Training should also be used to build comradery and make your employees feel invested. Take the time to show your employees not only how to do their jobs, but also how much their jobs means to you and your company.

Make your training stand out from the rest. Consider

unique training venues and/or giving your employees a personalized gift, such as a notebook, pen, shirt, or coffee mug, that is functional for the training and reminds them that you're invested in them as individuals.

However you conduct training, keep in mind the need to manage the expectations of your employees, because you're more likely to build a lasting relationship when you do.

Employee Contract

Texas, where our business resides, is what's called an "employee-at-will state," which means that you can terminate employees at any time and for any reason that does not directly conflict with the state's laws or an agreement otherwise. You don't have to have an agreement, but one may be appropriate to help manage the expectations of your employees.

In our state, an employee agreement may limit your ability to fire the employee absent an express violation of that agreement. Therefore, we've advised certain clients to use their employee handbook and job description to share expectations and forego creating an employment agreement.

However, for other employers, it may be appropriate to have an agreement, especially when the employer is seeking an employee for a certain period of time and has no intention of modifying any terms of the employment during that period.

If you decide to have an employee agreement, please have it legally reviewed to ensure that you don't inadvertently have any illegal terms in the contract. Those illegal terms could be used against you in an unemployment claim to your detriment.

Unemployment Claims

Unemployment claims can result in higher payroll taxes for your company. Therefore, you don't want them. Payroll taxes are like car insurance. Even if the accident wasn't your fault, if it's reported to your insurance, your car insurance will likely rise. Similarly, regardless of whether you're successful with the unemployment claim, your payroll tax could rise as a result of the claim.

It's best to be preventive in nature by managing expectations. However, if a claim is made against your company, you may want to consult an attorney for assistance, although legal representation is not required.

IT'S DUE SEASON!

I hope that reading this chapter has given you a true appreciation for the importance of rest and delegation. Don't be afraid to take breaks! Make sure that you delegate to trustworthy agents. When you decide that you're ready to hire, be sure to manage your employees' expectations to avoid unnecessary claims and litigation.

Remember to have faith! Hebrews 11:1 tells us that "faith is the substance of things hoped for, the evidence of things not seen" (KJV).

Now, let's plan your break! To help plan your next S. A. N. D. (which, as a reminder, stands for Sleep + Abandon + Nurture + Disconnect), ask yourself the following questions:

1. Who can cover for me in my absence?

2. If no one, how can I cover for myself? (Examples: automated out of office, updating my voicemail, posting a message on my website and social media that I'm currently unavailable)

3. How long do I want to rest?

4. Where do I want to rest?

6. With whom do I want to rest?

7. Who will care for my children while I rest? (Don't allow childcare to get in the way of your plans!)

8. What will I do on my vacation? (Don't forget to rest.)

9. How can people contact me in case of an emergency?

10. How can I prepare to be as inaccessible as possible?

11. What would stop me from resting? I'll take this one for you: *nothing!*

June Notes

July:
Freedom for Freedom's Sake

Shinia Lambert

...the things that divide us are far less important than those that connect us.[53]

—Rachel Naomi Remen

Freedom [noun]: the power or right to act, speak, or think as one wants without hindrance or restraint.[54]

When you think of freedom, especially in the context of business, what comes to mind? If you're drawing a blank, you're not alone. Many people have yet to consider what role freedom currently plays or ought to play in how they conduct business. In this chapter, I want to highlight an often-over-looked aspect of freedom: responsibility. In our businesses, we have the freedom and, therefore, inherent responsibility to acknowledge and address the following three things:

   1. Gender disparity (a key part of which requires

2. Social responsibility

3. Discrimination in the workplace

TRUE FREEDOM IS OTHERS-CENTERED

Freedom isn't an end in itself. After all, having freedom simply means that you have the opportunity to do something that you couldn't do otherwise. You still have to act on the opportunity.

It sounds almost too simple, doesn't it? But think about freedom from the perspective of having freedom in Christ. Jesus didn't save us and set us free just so we could bear His name and go to heaven. Yes, that's a great gift and benefit, for sure! But He has a purpose for our freedom right here on earth as we live out our daily lives and walk with Him each step of the way. When Jesus set us free, it was with the intention and understanding that we would be empowered and equipped to do what we couldn't do when we were enslaved to sin.

Similarly, the freedom afforded to us in America, our freedom to make decisions and express ourselves, is not given to us without purpose. The idea, the motivation, the inspiration behind freedom is that we will use it to do things that add value to others and contribute to the common good.

Freedom does not condescend. It does not enslave. It does not overpower. Freedom sets others free. Freedom stands up for those who cannot stand for themselves. Freedom produces peacemakers. Freedom advances advocacy. Freedom is power. But with freedom comes great responsibility.

HOW DOES FREEDOM AFFECT OUR BUSINESSES?

Freedom in business can look like diversity and inclusion—for example, addressing the disparity between men and women and the diversity, or lack thereof, of age and race in the workplace.

As Christian business owners, we must navigate this bright line that, honestly, doesn't always shine so brightly. We are to love everyone and be inclusive but, at the same time, not dim our light or hide it under a basket.

We by no means want to imply that this is always a clear path to travel. Conversations and decisions that incorporate ideas of gender, race, age, religious beliefs, and so forth are difficult ones to have and require empathy and compassion, which can be hard to find today.

Nevertheless, just because some people may not be doing it or haven't yet found a way to do it well doesn't mean that we have to be lumped in with that number. We're moms after all—is there really anything we cannot do?

One way we can grow more comfortable with talking about bias and assessing whether we suffer from some misplaced prejudices of our own is doing what Mellody Hobson suggests: "Invite people into your life that don't look like or think like you." [55]

I know a phenomenally impactful motivational speaker who is a pioneer for people of color and one of the most committed advocates I've ever met. She always puts issues that affect the Black community at the forefront, everything from education to the effects of systematic racism. The only problem is her approach—from her disposition, to her rhetoric, to her willingness to partner—which only appeals to people who look like her and think like she does.

So, while she is successful in drawing crowds of other educated and purposeful Black people, she misses out on opportunities to reach larger crowds and to impact the thinking of those who could benefit from a different approach or perspective. In the end, who is she influencing? Not as many people as she could be. She may be solidifying the thought process of an established group, but if change, diversity, or inclusion is her motivation, she is failing despite her well-intentioned methods.

Don't feel the need to have a political agenda before you begin your business. Just be aware that as an entrepreneur, you are a leader. You possess influence, and with that influence comes another opportunity to represent Christ well. One way we can do that is to embrace those who may be different from us. We may never do it perfectly, but we can strive to do it purposefully.

FREEDOM FROM GENDER DISPARITY

Another aspect of bias is gender disparity in the workforce. Here are some surprising and disheartening statistics:

- Fewer than 85 CEOs in the Fortune 500 are

women.[56]

- Only 27 percent of C-suite positions in media and entertainment are held by women.[57]

- Yet 80 percent of all purchasing decisions are made by women.[58]

As entrepreneurs who are also women and mothers, we can flip these statistics and create a more culturally and equitable representation of women in the marketplace, as both buyers and sellers.

It does not make logical sense that while women make most of the purchasing decisions within the home, we are entirely under-represented when it comes to determining what will be placed into the market. We may buy more, but what we buy is still limited to what men have pushed into the market.

Now, I want to be clear about something. I love men. I think that they are wonderful creations of God who have a unique and important role in life and culture. But I also recognize the value of a woman and her unique and important role—not just at home, but also in the marketplace. And because the latter role is so underutilized, I believe that we miss out on major opportunities to affect and direct the course of business for the better.

As you step out and start your own business, who knows what opportunities you may create for other women? Even if you don't create an actual employment position, your courage to step out in faith and start your business may encourage another woman to do the same and so on until the market is saturated with women offering unique and valuable goods, services, and programs to the world!

FREEDOM FROM POOR RELATIONAL MANAGEMENT

Whenever I'm having any kind of discussion regarding the roles of men and women in business or relationships, I can't help but think of Queen Esther. If you're not familiar with Esther, she is a Hebrew Cinderella, the "rags to riches" young woman who went from her cousin's home to the king's court. What we know now that Esther didn't at the time is that God positioned her in the royal court "for such a time as this" (Esther 4:14 KJV). She was there specifically to save her people. Although a queen, Esther, as a woman, had no outright influence or power. But as usual, it was the woman's responsibility to fix the mess!

Women are powerful vessels of influence and peacekeeping. It can be exhausting when we don't have the authority to make decisions, yet we are responsible for finding, creating, and executing solutions. Now more than ever, it is urgent for us to understand our God-given roles of entrepreneurship and womanhood.

I was scrolling on social media when I came across a meme that had been shared by an acquaintance of mine. The meme read something to the effect that men fear women who have their "stuff" together. A young man commented that women (I'm slightly paraphrasing here) who have their stuff together are "pushy and very detached" and use school or work as an excuse to be that way. He went on to elaborate that, historically, women naturally desired to be taken care of and protected by men, and when that element is gone, women start acting unnaturally and develop an alpha-male complex.

I know.

I know.

Take three deep breaths.

Where to begin? Let's unpack the initial statement first. Are men scared of women who have their stuff together? No, I don't believe that's the case. All men are not afraid of women who are successful. It's counterintuitive to believe that people are so dysfunctional that we run from what's good for us.

On the other hand, I do believe that there are men who can be intimidated by a woman's success—not because she's doing anything to *try* to intimidate them, but as the natural result of their own insecurities. I think that some men are intimidated by women who make more money than they do or who are highly educated, although neither of these things speaks directly to the quality of a person.

What is generally called "pushy and very detached" in a woman would be called assertive and ambitious in a man. The fact that prioritizing education or working hard is seen as something negative is jarring. I've never seen either reduce a woman's sincere interest in a quality man or relationship. I have seen a woman not be willing to settle for a subpar man. I've seen a woman not be willing to let someone jeopardize what she's worked hard to build. But I've never seen a woman

177

reject a quality man because she's successful or desires to be.

As a successful woman myself, I still desire to be treated like a woman and can admire and appreciate the uniqueness that God perfected in a man. But I throw flags on the play if being a successful woman means that I must somehow dim my light. That's called insecurity, and I'm not going to submit to it.

STRONG AS A MOTHER

How do we, whether single or married, find the right balance between being an entrepreneur and being a woman? Mind you, I don't think that men have to have this conversation. I don't think many books touch on how a man can be both an entrepreneur and masculine. Nevertheless, let's dive in.

I have a best friend who is a go-getter. She's a lawyer, a sole practitioner in her own firm, a mother, a daughter, a wife, a believer—an all-around amazing human being and my role model. In the last year, as we've been enduring our long-distance friendship, we have resorted to sending each other voice memos throughout the day. This became our solution to keep in touch when we both struggled to find free time to talk on the phone.

I was not at all surprised to receive a voice memo from her after her recent visit to the orthopedic doctor. Approximately two months prior to her appointment, she'd hit her foot and felt an intense pain over the next couple of days. My friend, wonder woman that she is, is also an avid runner. After giving herself a day or two to recover, she resumed running, even though she acknowledged that her foot hurt and she even limped at times. She kept right on running and lawyering and mothering and wife-ing and all the other "-ings" we do. Months later, my friend finally visited the doctor, who told her that her toe was, in fact, broken. My friend had been doing life at the same velocity as always, but with a broken appendage. Isn't that just like a woman?

No one told her that she couldn't go to the doctor. In fact, many of us encouraged her to do so. No one told her not to take time off or that her responsibilities could not be handled by someone else if she needed a break. But my friend, much like most of us who own businesses and are moms, didn't believe in prioritizing her own needs above the needs of others. Sometimes it's our family's expectations that weigh heavily on us or our children's, our business partners', or our employees'. Sometimes it's the pressure we put on ourselves. When it becomes too much, it's a sign that we may not be relating intelligently with ourselves or with others.

Think of this scenario for a minute. There are two executives in business, both of whom are ambitious, competent, and driven. Both are willing to work late hours and burn the midnight oil to see their businesses succeed. Both leave their respective offices, exhausted, and head home for the night. One gets home, throws the blazer on the back of the couch, grabs leftovers out of the fridge, eats in front of the TV, and then jumps in the shower and heads to bed. The other opens the door, hears feet pattering down the hall (*why aren't they in bed?*), and is immediately asked to help with homework or sign a permission slip. And, oh yeah, "We haven't eaten yet. Can you make your special spaghetti?"

Now, be honest. Do you envision the executive being a mother in the first scenario or the second? It's the second. Rarely will a woman who is a mother stop working when she leaves work; her responsibilities just shift to a new space.

Relational intelligence helps us to envision what a realistic day looks like for us and communicate that to others in order to help manage their expectations of us. At the core of relational intelligence is assessment—assessing the roles we play in the lives of others and vice versa, specifically the time, energy, and emotional commitment we devote to those roles. To assess whether we are relating intelligently, we need to be able to have some critical, sometimes uncomfortable, conversations.

Conversations regarding business and entrepreneurial pursuits are going to vary based on marital status and whether you have children, but below are some talking points to get you started:

1. Communicate about expectations. What do you expect from yourself and one another regarding how you manage your business and your family?

2. Communicate about goals. How do each of you (you and your partner or spouse) define success?

3. Communicate about growth. How would promotion or increased responsibilities at home or at work impact your relationship?

4. Communicate about the future. Consider mapping out a plan. Not everything will go according to your plan, but wise people start with one. Adjust if need be. Can you foresee any challenges that you can address now?

5. Communicate about preventative measures. Can you plan for how to address unexpected challenges in the future? What will you do, or even better, what will you *not do* (for example, get a divorce, dissolve the business, or take out a second mortgage on the home) in the event that the unexpected occurs?

6. Communicate about leadership. How can you each exert positive influence in and over this business venture? Do you only point out problems, or do you also bring solutions?

7. Communicate about your vision. Are you fully committed to your vision? Can you articulate that vision to your partner and family in a way that excites them to get on board? You can't expect other people to support a plan you're not fully behind.

8. Communicate about your relationship and family. Are you each committed to keeping your marriage first? If you have children, how involved will they be in the business, if at all?

9. Communicate about adaptation. Are you willing to assess what is or isn't working and adapt when necessary?

Besides addressing gender disparity, which requires relational intelligence, demonstrating freedom in our businesses involves taking social responsibility, engaging in our communities (locally, nationally, and internationally), and being aware of the biblical principles encouraging us to use our freedom to help others.

FREEDOM AND SOCIAL RESPONSIBILITY

We touched on this briefly in the May chapter when we referenced how certain businesses give back or create programs that allow for their production of goods to benefit the community—a reward system for buying their products, if you will. Here I want us to think more about how we, as individuals in business, can create environments that reflect the love of God in responsible ways.

For example, when George Floyd was tragically murdered, Ebony and I were extremely affected. We are both Black women living in America and were enduring what seemed like an overwhelming season of Black deaths at the hands of police officers here in the country we love, the same country our families have served for generations (Ebony personally having served and having a husband currently serving in the United States Army). On top of all that, we are both mothers of Black boys, so the impact was excruciating for us, though that word doesn't seem like enough to describe how we felt.

While all of that was happening in our own lives and in our country, we were also active business owners, serving clients whom we might disagree with politically, religiously, or socially. We had to decide how were we going to express our despair as individuals and as a business.

There was no doubt in our minds that we had to say something, although let me be clear: silence is a statement, and it was one we were "hearing" from far too many colleagues, friends, and even clients. Ebony and I had to realign our priorities and reassess business relationships because the silence was deafening, especially from those who said they cared about us and shared our same foundational beliefs. We just didn't understand how these dear friends, colleagues, and partners could not say anything publicly about what had happened and how it affected our community. But more importantly, what were we going to say?

Ebony had the brilliant idea that we could make a simple yet impactful statement to our customers and our community via our social media: "Injustice is Illegal." It was something that everyone could agree with, and how they defined injustice would be up to them. This brings me to a very important matter. If you are going to take a stance on something, it needs to be authentic.

After the second round of sad events that led to the re-emergence of the Black Lives Matter movement, I'll admit that I was cynical about the companies that showed support via their advertisements and social media. Why? Because it felt disingenuous. Why did it take the unwarranted deaths of

Black people in America to draw this sudden support? Where was the contribution to awareness and advocacy programs to help bolster and build awareness before the bullets struck people down? For me, it felt like the age-old capitalistic opportunity to sell more products or increase web traffic.

But this also taught me an important lesson. No matter what message my business puts out, whether audible or visual, the positive culture we cultivate or the compassionate customer service we provide, someone is always going to be unhappy. Some people will see and believe that we are authentic, and some will doubt and question. Some will stand in solidarity with us, and others would rather see us fall. That's the nature of living in a free world; it includes the freedom to see, believe, think, and act differently. It's a gift and a curse. Nevertheless, it's a reminder.

Whatever your message is, whether it's the popular opinion or not, be willing to stand ten toes down on it. Is that social media post, comment, rant, or promotional skit on TikTok a mountain you are willing to die on? It sounds dramatic, I know, but in the age of cancel culture, all it takes is one comment and the internet is unleashed!

In June 2022, Harry E. Reed Insurance Co., a small business in Millinocket, Maine, experienced this backlash firsthand. Shortly ahead of the Juneteenth holiday, Melanie Higgins, the daughter (and sole employee) of the owner, posted a sign with the following on the business doors: "Juneteenth, it's whatever ... we're closed. Enjoy your fried chicken and collard greens." [59]

Juneteenth is a recently recognized federal holiday that

commemorates June 19, 1865, the day slaves in Texas finally learned that they'd been emancipated, nearly three years following the Emancipation Proclamation. It didn't take much of a stretch to connect the small business's remarks to long-held stereotypes regarding African Americans and fried chicken (but on a sidenote, who doesn't like fried chicken?).

Social media came in like a wrecking ball and shared pictures of the sign over 10,000 times! As a result, not only was the small business flooded with calls and poor business reviews, but Progressive and Allstate, two of the nation's largest insurance carriers, terminated their relationship with Harry E. Reed Insurance Co., which clearly will affect their ability to garner the same client base and backing they once enjoyed.

Here's the moral of the story. You are free to express your opinions about people, places, or things in whatever manner you choose. What you don't have the freedom to do is choose the consequences. While we've all said things we wish we could take back, the age of the internet makes retracting those statements impossible. Don't risk being cancelled over a comment you could have kept to yourself.

Furthermore, if you don't sincerely believe in a cause, movement, or agenda , don't pretend like you do. Those who are genuinely invested in those causes, movements, and agendas will be able to tell that you are pretending and using their passion as a marketing tool. In other words, in those moments, let's reject Nike's advice and just *don't* do it.

In the world we live in today, it's nearly impossible to operate our businesses in a vacuum, nor should we want to. As believers, we are called to be difference makers and do what we can to engage in what's going on around us. If you find yourself or your business in a space that is difficult to navigate, here are some things you can do internally:

- Call a meeting to discuss any current events that may be imposing upon or affecting your business's culture, community, or mission. Suggest ways you would like employees to respond when acting as representatives of the company.

- Offer to bring in a mental-health professional to meet with employees who may have difficulty exploring or articulating their emotions because of what has occurred.

- Allow for an open-door policy for reporting.

- Swiftly address offensive and harmful rhetoric or behavior, complying with your company's policies and procedures.

There are some external things you can do as well:

- Educate yourself about current issues by conducting your own research and developing an informed opinion that you can articulate intelligently and lovingly. Acknowledge impactful events in a tasteful and non-adversarial way.

- Have fruitful conversations with individuals within your networking groups, purposeful partnerships, and relationships that matter.

- Clearly communicate your ethics and beliefs to your clients or customer base without being exclusionary or divisive toward those whose beliefs may differ from yours. This would be a great opportunity to invest in a social or public relations specialist who can help you to craft content and responses to sensitive and/or urgent issues.

What Does God Expect from Us?

There are biblical implications when it comes to freedom, and these affect our businesses as well. Galatians 5:13 reads, "For you have been called to live in freedom, my brothers and sisters. But don't use your freedom to satisfy your sinful nature. Instead, use your freedom to serve one another in love" (NLT). God expects us to use our freedom to serve others in love.

Considering that you were set free to make a difference, honestly ask yourself the following questions:

- Do I have any biases or prejudices that keep me from serving freely through my life and business?

- Do I treat potential clients differently based on their race, religious affiliation, or sexual orientation?

- Am I using my faith as a sword of superiority instead of an olive branch of peace?

- Have I neglected to speak up for those who don't have a voice?

- How can I be a good steward of the freedom that's been given to me?

First Peter 2:16–17 reads, "For you are free, yet you are God's slaves, so don't use your freedom as an excuse to do evil. Respect everyone, and love the family of believers. Fear God, and respect the king" (NLT).

Use your freedom—your position and ability to be an entrepreneur—to do good and show respect to everyone, especially those in the family of believers.

FREEDOM FROM DISCRIMINATION

Business owners who want to create an open, transparent work culture and environment that is mindful of diversity and prohibits discrimination, bias, and offensive behavior need to have appropriate policies and guidelines, which can be incorporated into an employee handbook and training as discussed in the June chapter.

Where to Begin

Honestly, for the most part, we rarely encounter clients who intentionally desire to offend or discriminate or encourage that kind of behavior in their workplace. That doesn't change the fact that an employee was offended or discriminated against.

Often employers and small-business owners are ignorant about what they can or can't ask, say, or imply. One of the ways we have tried to assist our clients is starting with the interview process, before an employee–employer relationship begins. It is possible, even as well intentioned as you may be, that you may ask questions that you are legally prohibited from asking, even if you never take that information into consideration when choosing to hire or not to hire.

Topics to avoid include:

- Age
- Race, ethnicity, or color
- Gender or sex
- Country of national origin or birthplace
- Religion
- Disability
- Marital or family status or pregnancy

I would say that these topics are commonly considered red flags and you want to avoid them at all costs. However, if the interviewee initiates conversation about any of the topics above or below, just make sure that you handle them with consideration and tact. If there has been significant discussion in any of the areas above or below, I would recommend ending the interview with something like: "I've sincerely enjoyed such a pleasant conversation with you about your [origin, pregnancy, gender, etc.], but I want to be clear that I can't consider any of those things during the hiring process." Cover yourself by communicating that fact clearly.

Some questions that have gotten people into trouble in the past are:

- What arrangements are you able to make for child-care while you work?

- How old are your children?

- When did you graduate from high school?

- Are you a U. S. citizen?

- What does your wife do for a living?

- Where did you live while you were growing up?

- Will you need personal time for a particular religious holiday?

- Are you comfortable working for a female boss?

- There is a large disparity between your age and that of the position's co-workers. Is this a problem for you?

- How long do you plan to work until you retire?

- We believe in promoting diversity. What race are you?

- Our firm believes heavily in family. Are you married, or do you plan to be?

When Ebony and I interviewed for administrative assistants, we knew that we couldn't ask the applicants, "Are you a Christian?" although we are very vocal about both being believers and establishing our firm on the foundation of our

Christian beliefs. Instead, we would ask something like, "Some of our clients own churches and have specific religious beliefs. Would it be offensive to you to assist clients whose religious beliefs may differ from yours?" We want to attract, hire, and retain employees who believe not only that they are chosen, but that this is a place they truly feel called to be and feel comfortable being. That comes with a mutual respect that encourages open and transparent (yet legal!) communication right from the beginning.

Whom to Protect

There are federal statutes that prohibit employment discrimination against members of protected classes: race, color, religion, national origin, gender, age, and disability. In addition, many states have their own employment discrimination laws, which may offer more protection than the federal statutes do.

Title VII of the Civil Rights Act of 1964, which is the most important statute prohibiting both intentional and unintentional employment discrimination based on race, color, national origin, religion, or gender, applies to employers with fifteen or more employees and labor unions with fifteen or more members.

Title VII also prohibits employers from discriminating against employees based on their employees' religion. Employers cannot treat their employees poorly or more favorably based on their religious beliefs and/or practices and must also reasonably accommodate the religious practices of its employees unless doing so would cause undue hardship.

What to Include

Discrimination and sexual harassment policies can and should include the following:

1. A clear statement that the company prohibits employee discrimination of any kind, including sexual harassment, emphasizing that the behavior is prohibited regardless of who the intended victim is (an employee, manager, vendor, or customer)

2. Definitions of *discrimination* and *sexual harassment*

3. An outline of prohibited behavior with an acknowledgment that the list may not be exhaustive

4. An outline of the disciplinary procedure and steps if someone violates the discrimination or harassment policies

5. Whether there will be a duty to report such behavior for anyone who observes, overhears, witnesses, or is involved in it

6. How complaints will be handled

7. What resources are available for the individual who alleges discrimination or sexual harassment and whose allegations are confirmed

8. A clear statement that retaliation against anyone claiming discrimination or harassment is prohibited

Although these policies can be included in the employee handbook, which your employees will generally sign to say that they received it, I believe these policies to be of such importance that there should be a signature line on each of the policies within the handbook. Alternatively, consider printing them on a separate page and having the employees sign it. Make sure to give them a copy and keep the original in each employee's file.

I know that this chapter was a little heavier than others, but we cannot deny the times we are living in and the propensity for offense. As believers who have been entrusted with this special space of influence called entrepreneurship, we must remember that we are the ones called to do life differently—abundantly and better. It is important to do a self-assessment often to determine if prejudices, biases, or even an aversion to diversity has crept into our hearts. Self-awareness is essential. Awareness precedes improvement. Once we know where we are, we can grow, and isn't growth a good thing?

IT'S DUE SEASON!

Stating that it can be hard to identify our biases and prejudices is putting it mildly. We all have varied backgrounds, upbringings, and experiences that influence and affect how we see life and others. Growth requires addressing those areas of ourselves that aren't always pretty or praiseworthy. Let's do the hard work of uprooting anything that might get in the way of us living, serving, and loving at our optimal capacity.

I want to challenge you this month to take an Implicit Association Test (otherwise known as an IAT). The test (which can be found through a simple Google search), reveals any implicit biases you may have that you aren't even aware of. If you're surprised by your results and are willing to share, we'd love to hear from you. Check in with our online community on Facebook at CapitalMoms: Creating Powerful and Passionate Mom Entrepreneurs.

Let's end with this simple prayer from Psalm 139:23–24 (NIV):

Search me, God, and know my heart; test me and know my anxious thoughts. See if there is any offensive way in me, and lead me in the way everlasting.

Amen.

July Notes

_____

_____

_____

_____

_____

_____

_____

_____

_____

_____

_____

_____

_____

_____

_____

_____

_____

August:
Back to School —
Continuing Education

Shinia Lambert

Growth and comfort do not co-exist.[60]

—David J. Schwartz

Knowledge [noun]: facts, information, and skills acquired by a person through experience or education; the theoretical or practical understanding of a subject.[61]

If there is anything I'm familiar with, especially as an attorney, it's continuing education. Not only do we have to complete a minimum of seven years of post-high-school education, but we are also required to complete courses annually that keep us aware of the current laws, policies, and ethics in our respective fields of practice. Yes, ethics. Did you just recall a lawyer joke in your head? Be nice!

Regardless of your level of education, the idea behind this chapter is that you, your business, and your clients are best served when:

- You are educated about your field, service, or product.

- You can acknowledge the areas where you need to grow.

- You are willing to take advantage of available resources.

THE BLESSING OF LIFELONG LEARNING

In the Gospel of Mark, Jesus touched a blind man and asked, "'Do you see anything?' And he looked up and said, 'I see people, but they look like trees, walking'" (Mark 8:23–24 ESV). Jesus then touched the man a second time, and the man's sight was completely restored.

You may be thinking, *"What does a blind man have to do with continuing education?"* I'm glad you asked. As mothers and business owners, we are often strapped for time. This means that anything we commit to not only has to pass the importance test, but also must be something worthy of our limited time and resources. Let's face it: as mothers, we often come last on the list of what is important! Rarely do we grant time to ourselves, even though we are more than worthy of doing so.

As a result, it can take a lot of convincing to embrace continuing education, which doesn't always seem necessary, important, or worthy of our time. So why pursue continuing education? The answer, simply put, is to avoid the trap of mediocrity. Most of us can say, "The job is getting done. We're making money. We're doing okay." Yet, if we're honest, we might admit that we're settling, that we're reluctantly accepting less than what we want or deserve.

Let's get back to the story of the blind man's healing. Since the blind man said that he saw people who "look like trees, walking" (Mark 8:24 ESV), we can safely assume that he wasn't born blind. If he had been, how would he have known what trees or people looked like?

Think about this for a moment. This man lost his sight completely, and after one touch, he could see *something*. Okay, stop right there. There are many people who would be fine with seeing *something*, because something is better than what they had. But notice that with a second touch, the man was completely healed. There's so much we could unpack here that it could be a book all by itself! However, what we need to see right now is that sometimes to be complete, we must give it a second go. Sometimes we need that extra touch or to be willing to take that extra step.

It all begins with our willingness to be honest about where we are in life. Imagine if the man had been so excited about seeing *something* that he had made *something* synonymous with being fully healed! Imagine if he'd been willing to stop there because seeing *something* was better than seeing nothing. Imagine if he'd been willing to settle.

The Comfortable Cage of Complacency

What in your business have you been willing to accept because it's better than nothing? What's your *something*? What could exponentially increase your market, your revenue, your visibility, or your knowledge if you were to give it a second look, a second touch? Are we willing to admit that we could be better?

That's what continuing education is about for a CapitalMom. It's about acknowledging areas where you need to grow and embracing that as an opportunity to be your best self.

This isn't judgment or punishment, and it's certainly not a rebuke. People who think highly of themselves invest in themselves. Beginning that process requires a serious self-assessment. I recommend spending some quiet time mapping out exactly where you and your business stand. Here are some questions to get you started:

- What are some trends I'm seeing in my revenue?

- What are some areas where I'd like to see growth and expansion?

- What positive and negative feedback have I received from clients?

- What are my customer service standards, and are they being met consistently?

- What are my goals for the next year, three years, five years, and so on?

There are no right or wrong answers. It's your business and your assessment. But remember that it's more than just your business. It's your calling and your God-given vision. No one else can see it like you can, which means no one can execute it like you can, either. This doesn't mean that you decline the input and advice of trusted colleagues and counselors. In fact, later in this chapter, we'll discuss the value of mentors. However, it does mean that even after receiving their counsel, you must decide what you will implement and how that will look for you, your business, and those who depend on you, such as your employees, clients, and family.

HOW CAN WE INSPIRE INNOVATION?

It is always important to consider ways we could be working smarter and not harder. That's an intriguing concept, right? It implies that we need to be doing something differently. *Differently* implies change, and change can be disruptive. Any successful business is going to have a culture and an environment that welcome creativity and innovation.

Creativity and innovation arrive on the heels of a willingness to admit that things could be better, a type of vulnerability that allows us to be stretched and challenged. In *Daring Greatly*, Dr. Brené Brown wrote, "Learning and creating are inherently vulnerable...." [62]

We don't have to be afraid of innovative ideas. Instead, we should welcome them and apply them in ways that are beneficial to our businesses.

Whether you operate your business all alone or serve a

host of staff and employees, how you respond to opportunities to gain experience and explore innovative ideas sends a message that cannot be ignored. If you're open and welcoming, you can create space to imagine endless possibilities and ways to apply them that increase your ability to serve others with quality services or products.

What if the opposite is true? What if you're inadvertently cultivating a culture in which new ideas are shunned or discouraged in the spirit of "don't fix what's not broken"? If that's the case, you'll not only risk losing valuable staff and stifling creativity, but you may lose your vision altogether.

Check In with Your Creativity

Where are you on the spectrum of creativity and innovation? Ask yourself:

1. Am I open to educating myself regularly about what's happening in my field and my market? If not, what is it I'm afraid of discovering?

2. Am I creating a space for myself and others to think creatively and outside of the box, or am I simply trying to recreate what I've seen others accomplish?

3. Do I welcome input from those I trust?

4. Do I become defensive when presented with other perspectives?

5. Can I see and support the value in a different approach, even if it's not the one I chose or would have originally been drawn to?

6. Can I handle and provide constructive feedback?

7. Am I still excited about what I've started?

8. Am I engaged in my business, or have I begun going through the motions?

9. Do I use shame, humiliation, or public correction to dissuade the presentation of innovative ideas?

10. Do I feel insecure about my continuing education?

11. If I'm hesitant to step out and voice or welcome a new opinion or stretch myself to learn, what messages might I have been fed as a child, an employee, or a spouse that affect my willingness to speak up or learn?

12. Do I have a safe, judgment-free space to share these feelings and to be supported as I work through them?

It's important to do this self-evaluation regularly. Many business owners share stories of feeling stuck yet are anxious about what it would take to propel them forward. Don't let the anxiety associated with change prevent you from being self-aware. We cannot improve and grow until we know the reality of where we are. But also understand that not every attempt at growth needs to be huge. It just needs to be intentional and purposeful.

SELF-LEADERSHIP ACCELERATES GROWTH

Self-leadership is the highest form of leadership. Your influence on yourself is ten times stronger than your influence on anyone else or other people's influence on you. You can begin shaping that influence by participating in practices that help you to grow personally and purposefully.

When I committed to a journey of growth, which included but wasn't exclusive to my business, I started with baby steps. I committed to reading two non-fiction books a month related to interpersonal relationships, leadership, or conflict resolution. This simple step gave me insight into how others thought, how I could better organize and execute my own ideas, and how I could contribute and add value to the lives and successes of others in the ways that they needed, rather than only what I was comfortable giving. It encouraged me to think outside of the box and presented me with opportunities to trust God in new and exciting ways. It began with a commitment to reading and developed into a commitment to learning, understanding, and applying this knowledge in various areas.

Small steps can be barrier breakers. You simply need to start.

Maybe you're ready for a bigger challenge, and while you can appreciate taking smaller steps, you're promptly positioned to propel forward. This step may look like enrolling in a marketing course or a creative writing class at the local college. It could be finishing a degree or mustering up the bravery to start one. It could mean hiring more experienced staff, providing your employees with innovative training, joining your city's chamber of commerce, networking with potential mentors in your field, or seeking ways to partner with other businesses that share your vision.

The options are endless. It's about being willing to admit that you can and should always be improving, that at the core of who we, as believers, are is the idea that we are transforming daily into the likeness of Christ. That transformation implies that we cannot stay the same.

Acceleration doesn't happen by accident. If you want to be equipped and prepared for success and transformation, you need to be engaged. You need to make deliberate decisions that affect the direction and course of your life instead of letting life happen to you and agreeing to make the best of it.

Self-sabotage and complacency are real. I would go so far as to say that they are often tools the enemy uses to keep us from being all that God would have us be. We can be well intentioned, intelligent, and capable, but if we do not execute, acceleration and elevation are not possible. We cannot become better without doing better. Read that carefully. I didn't say "doing more." I said "doing better."

This doesn't mean that your trajectory looks like anyone else's. We never intend to infer that good personal and business practices ought to be applied in a cookie-cutter fashion across the board. We hope that everything we share with you brings value, but we also understand that how that value manifests in your life, your business, and your family is unique to you. And we implore and encourage you to embrace that uniqueness.

Comparison is the killer of many callings. You have the God-given authority and ability to seek out what is for you and reject what isn't—without judgment, of course!

THE MYTHS THAT DISRUPT
OUR GROWTH AND SUCCESS

Growth may take time, effort, and some adjusting, but it doesn't have to be a grind or a struggle. There are three big myths that women may buy into that can impede their growth and block their path to success. The first myth is that any form of change in your life must include sacrifice. The second myth is that change must be tough. And the third is that change will eventually come to you.

Myth 1: Change Must Include Sacrifice

We need to release the belief that every step toward becoming a better version of ourselves requires sacrifice. That's a lie, and it's been used throughout history to control women. It causes entrepreneurs (who are also mothers and wives) to resist investing in themselves because they have been told that it automatically means someone else has to suffer as a result. As a CapitalMom, you understand the value of investing in yourself. You do so because you think highly of yourself. Never forget:

- You are worth the effort!

- You are worth the commitment!

- You are worth enjoying the process!

Oh, and never feel guilty about it!

Myth 2: Change Must Be Tough

Another barrier to growth that we sometimes face is the idea that change must be hard. I'll openly confess that I am resistant to change. Unfortunately, I have allowed seasonal cycles to repeat in my life for years because the idea of change—not even the change itself, just the *idea* of it— caused so much anxiety.

Does that sound familiar to you? Has anyone else been lulled into complacency by your comfort zone? Again, no judgment. But if we are going to operate in excellence and continue growing and evolving, it's going to require us to become comfortable with change.

Myth 3: Change Will Eventually Come to Us

We shouldn't postpone living an awesome life until change finds us. Don't wait for an unexpected call to propel you forward. Don't wait for an email that will transform your life to land in your inbox. We should meet change head-on.

First, this requires us to be willing to admit that something needs to change, and that can be hard to accept. Second, we sometimes tell ourselves that if something needs to change, we must be doing something wrong. It couldn't be further from the truth. The acknowledgment that a change needs to occur is an indication that things are shifting. We can choose to shift with them and grow or settle and stagnate.

Do you remember when Jesus told His disciples the Parable of the Talents (Matthew 25:14–30)? There was a master who had three servants, and before he left to go on a trip, he gave five talents (millions of dollars in today's currency) to the first servant, two to the second, and one to the last. When he returned, he met with his servants to see what they had done with the talents he had left them.

The first servant, who was given five talents, doubled his investment and brought back five more. The second servant also doubled his investment and brought back two more. But the servant who had been given one had nothing to show for the time his master had been gone. Why? Because he was afraid to take a risk. As a result, the servant wasted not only time, but the opportunity he had been given to steward.

Change and growth inherently contain an element of risk, but with no risk, there's no reward. The servant who did nothing with what was entrusted to him had his one talent taken away while the other servants were given even more to steward. Let's not miss the chance to double our investment, whether it be time, energy, money, or whatever else God wants to multiply in our businesses, because we're afraid of change.

Why Networking Is Necessary
for Effective Entrepreneurship

Networking is a wonderful opportunity to meet other business owners and to introduce yourself to your local community. Most networking groups function as small, cooperative communities in which members do their best to utilize one another's services and assist with making referrals for one another. These referrals help to bring in new business as members of the networking group encounter potential clients whose needs other members may be able to meet. Not all networking opportunities or groups are the same. Some require dues or have attendance requirements. We highly encourage you to begin by attending a large variety to determine the best fit for you.

When Ebony and I began our partnership, we registered as members in two nationally recognized and well-known networking groups. Both groups consisted of great people who offered services or goods to the public and had proven to be committed to building relationships with one another and supporting each other's businesses.

Over time, we found that, based on our professional niche, one of the networking groups wasn't the best fit for us. Referrals were limited, and we found ourselves struggling to go to weekly midday meetings that cut into the time we could be scheduling consultations, so we decided to discontinue our membership in that networking group. However, the relationships we built in that group carried on, and we still recommend many of the businesses that we have come to know and love.

While the purpose of networking is marketed as gaining more clients, at the heart of it, there ought to be a sincere desire to build relationships. Those relationships allow you to get to know other business owners—the quality of their work, their work ethic, their intentions—and then make referrals as you come across people who might benefit from their services. True networking cannot be successful without the foundation of genuine relationships. When you come into networking environments with the right motives and intentions, you never have to be afraid of leaving those groups or organizations if they no longer serve you, because the underlying relationships remain. There are ways to depart gracefully and still value the people who remain in those groups when you choose to move along to better opportunities for you and your business.

Also be aware of networking opportunities that may not appear obvious or are not marketed as such. For example, every time you go out, you ought to have your business card on you, or you may want to consider a digital business card for ease of use. You never know whom you might meet at the grocery store, the local park while your kids play, or standing in line to buy that fabulous new pair of shoes.

Conversations can strike up anywhere, and once you begin talking, what you do for a living is an inevitable topic. Be ready not only to discuss what you do, but also to let others know how to reach you if they want to take the next step and do business.

One area that Ebony and I believe is an untapped opportunity for small businesses to network also happens to be a place most of us frequent at least once a week: church! As advocates and participants in small-business and mom ministries, we believe that they prove fruitful for networking and spiritual growth. If your church doesn't already have one or both ministries, consider advocating for them with your church's board. Don't forget to recommend this book as a great resource to get started!

The Fruit of Networking

My business partner is the queen of in-person networking. Ebony makes it a point to be active in the community and to engage with causes that matter. She has a huge heart for our community and loves to contribute in any way she can, especially when it comes to celebrating and supporting other small businesses. I enjoy social networking online, creating and posting thoughtful content that leads others to engage in impactful ways. It's important to acknowledge the success of others, and in an era when social media is a major player in marketing, I can support a wide net of small businesses both locally and globally.

Giftedness is a blessing, and it's not humility to hide what you are naturally inclined to do well. Rather, the underutilization of that skill could stifle your personality and creativity. Networking is a skill. If you have a partner or staff member who is naturally inclined to network and socialize, harness that positive energy.

Also consider thinking outside of the box and using one of your greatest resources, friends and family, to its highest potential. For example, my mother naturally has the gift of hospitality, and she makes the most beautiful invitations, cards, and wrapped gifts. She made invitations for our grand opening and coffee mugs for our proof party! Ebony's younger sister is by far the most helpful and industrious person I know. She can and is willing to do whatever it takes to get the job done (and will make you laugh the entire time).

Who has a special gift in your circle that you haven't considered? Does your son have a knack for creating TikToks? Let him manage your social media account and task him with posting a few videos a week. Does your best friend write well? Ask her to oversee your monthly newsletter. Get busy getting creative!

If you are currently in business alone and don't feel naturally gifted in the area of networking, I recommend starting small. Begin with circles of people you know well and branch out from there. Don't despise small beginnings. Remember that networking is about relationships and release yourself from the pressure to sell.

If you're thinking, *"Shai, I can't. I really don't feel comfortable speaking to people."* Okay. First, I'm going to recommend that you sign up for a CapitalMoms coaching session. In the meantime, let's delegate. If you can't network, due to a lack of interest, ability, or time, then consider paying someone to network for you, whether that's attending networking groups on your behalf or marketing for you online. There's a way to get it done. In words attributed to inventor and entrepreneur Thomas Edison, "When you have exhausted all possibilities, remember this—you haven't."

CULTIVATE YOUR NEGOTIATION SKILLS

Negotiating is an important skill to learn because it contributes to your ability as a woman and a business owner to advocate strongly for yourself among peers, both in your professional development and for your presence in the marketplace. Learning to negotiate is a beneficial tool because it also helps you to learn conflict resolution and critical thinking skills, which are worthwhile no matter what kind of business you own. Being a good negotiator requires learning to communicate effectively, which includes the artful craft of listening.

I know, I know, we have such important things to say, and if people would just listen to us, then they'd be fine. I get it. I really do. But negotiating forces us to consider what the other party needs, wants, or thinks is important. A successful negotiation attributes value to those things and finds a way for both parties to leave the table feeling like they've won.

THE IMPORTANCE OF MENTORING

To reach our highest potential, we should seek to operate from a place of peace. I don't mean an "if the day goes well and my kids don't get on my nerves" type of peace, because how often does that actually happen? I mean the supernatural, all-surpassing peace that Jesus promised would be ours as believers.

We can't operate from a place of peace if we are unsure of our steps moving forward. We are not perfect, nor do we have everything figured out. But we can position ourselves to receive information that allows us to make better choices regarding how we spend our time, gifts, and other resources.

One of the greatest decisions you can make in your life is allowing yourself to be mentored by someone who can pour richly into you, giving you access to information you would not otherwise have or would have to spend years gathering and filtering.

Mentoring Relationships Can Be Challenging

I can already tell that you might be giving me some resistance. I get it. Let's talk about it. There are several reasons why we might resist the idea of a mentor.

First, it can be hard to know whom to trust. That's fair. Sometimes the idea of selecting a mentor can feel overwhelming, especially if someone has offered his or her services to you or proposed mentoring you. If no one has offered, how do you ask? How do you submit to someone whom you don't know very well yet? How do you know if someone will lead you in the right direction? What if it's another fraud or scheme to get your money? Yes, good mentors can require payment. Don't be averse to paying someone to teach you personally the things you need to know.

Second, we may resist mentorship because we see it as one more person pointing out what we're doing wrong. We are afraid of being vulnerable, of someone knowing our weaknesses and potentially exploiting them. But that's not a healthy mentoring relationship, and I don't believe that it's the most common type, either.

A healthy relationship will point out where you need to grow and also teach you how. A great mentor will celebrate what you're doing right and continue to encourage you as you progress.

Everyone needs a mentor. We all need a guide to show us the way. Don't be ashamed to say that you don't know something. There's no shame in a lack of wisdom. There's far more to lose by choosing to remain unwise once you know that you need to grow in an area.

Five Kinds of Mentors to Seek Out in Your Life

To be genuinely happy and successful in life, I believe that you shouldn't limit yourself to one mentor.

Mentor 1: The Holy Spirit

For believers, the Holy Spirit is our first and primary mentor. It is the Holy Spirit's job to guide us and to teach us, so you've had a mentor ever since you became a believer! Does the Holy Spirit care about whether you start a business, excel in business, and grow in your business? Absolutely. If you've never entertained the idea of viewing the Holy Spirit as a mentor or even considered that God cares about your business, spend time in specific and strategic prayer regarding your work. A former pastor of mine often challenged us to ask the Holy Spirit to show us what we may need to start doing, stop doing, or change in order to join Him in what He is doing around us. I challenge you to do the same.

Mentor 2: Jesus

Let's not forget that Jesus demonstrated for us what being the ultimate mentor looks like. The Bible tells us in Hebrews 4:15 that Jesus can "empathize with our weaknesses" because He was "tempted in every way, just as we are," yet He never sinned (NIV). Jesus was also intentional about the company He kept, demonstrating that there are levels within the mentor relationship. He invested in everyone, but the investment varied based on the level of intimacy. Jesus had a large following, then the twelve disciples, then the inner circle of Peter, James, and John.

Mentor 3: Spiritual Mentor

I encourage you to seek out a spiritual mentor who aligns with your belief system. This mentor, who may or may not be an entrepreneur, will be invested in seeing you grow spiritually. Our spiritual health and intelligence affect everything else we do. As we grow in our relationship with God, that intimacy increases, and we can more clearly hear His voice. Not all of us know how to do that, and while the Holy Spirit is certainly capable of teaching us, we were designed for relationship. (Side note: you cannot escape relationship. I'm an introvert. I have tried.) While our relationship with God is primary, we need human faces, minds, hands, and hearts that we can see and touch. We need people who can relate to us, empathize with us, and challenge us.

Mentor 4: Business Mentor

You should also have a business mentor who operates a successful business, which may or may not be in your field. This person may or may not share your spiritual views or have your same personality type. Be willing to learn from those who are not like you. You can select what you will and won't take from people. You can admire someone's tenacity but not share his or her views on politics. You can learn from someone's business model without sharing religious views. There is a human commonality that you cannot ignore. And never neglect your opportunity to be an influencer.

Mentor 5: Relational Mentor

Last but not least, I recommend a relational mentor. This is someone, often a therapist, who can help you to navigate personal and professional relationships. Your relational mentor will be an unbiased third party to the relationship who can help you to see yourself clearly, set and enforce appropriate boundaries, and honor those with whom you are in relationship.

These professionals can teach us how to be transparent

and have those critical, sometimes uncomfortable conversations with others. They also teach us how to relate in a healthy way to ourselves. Therapists tend to help us focus on healing from our past. Life coaches are individuals who help us to move forward. If you can find both in one person, excellent. Otherwise, this may be an opportunity to employ two different individuals, understanding that they have a different focus, expertise, and end game.

It Can't Be All About You

I would be remiss if I didn't mention the importance of not only vetting and obtaining mentors for yourself, but also understanding the value you bring as a mentor. Just because you don't know everything doesn't mean that you don't have something to offer someone else who may need a little guidance along the way.

While Ebony and I seek to mentor our general counsel clients as we help them to frame, establish, and grow their businesses, we know that we can't do that one-on-one with everyone. But we can provide a guide to help show others the way. That's the heart of this whole book!

With that in mind, I invite you to ask yourself:

- To whom can I be a spiritual mentor?

- To whom can I be a business mentor?

- To whom can I be a relational mentor?

IT'S DUE SEASON!

Here's an affirmation that captures the essence of this chapter: *I commit to growing in knowledge, wisdom, and understanding. I will be open to being taught and challenged. I will not hinder what God wants to do in my life with thoughts like "It's too hard," "I'll never understand this," or "I give up." I receive all that God intends to deposit into me, and I will be a good steward of all that has been entrusted to me.*

If you're really motivated and ready to grow, here are some practical steps you can start today:

- *Read* ten pages of a non-fiction book per day. The book should focus on an area where you are trying to grow.

- *Journal* at the beginning or conclusion of each day. The means and method are up to you. Allow this to be a place where you can assess, evaluate, and reflect on what you want to accomplish or have accomplished in the day. I personally find it more satisfying to reflect at the end of the day. You'll find that you've been much more productive than you thought you were!

- *Commune with God* each day. Don't worry yourself with a specific amount of time spent; just allow yourself quiet time with God to seek His will and to refresh your soul. There are many free resources online you can use. If you need help getting started, please consider listening to my podcast "Rooted: Real People, Real Issues, Real Growth," which can be found on Apple podcast, Anchor, and Spotify!

August Notes

PART FOUR: AUTUMN

September:
*Em*bracing the Fall

Ebony Todd

To be prepared is half the victory.[63]
—Miguel de Cervantes

Embrace [verb]: to accept something or someone willingly, whether physically, mentally, or emotionally.

ARE YOU A "FALLER"?

As a child, I was a certified "faller." Though I was clumsy at times and had my fair share of trips, I'm not sure why I had so many embarrassing falls. I still have a large scar in the shape of a *W* (I prefer to call it a butterfly) from chasing a boy in middle school. Even though I didn't know how to prevent my falls, I always braced myself for them!

Shouldn't we all be prepared for the inevitable "falls" we will encounter in our lifetime?

Alright, lovely, we've talked about the soft and easy subjects, but now I need you to brace yourself for the toughest yet.

There are two things we can be certain of in this life:

1. We will all have challenges.

2. We will all pass away.

That leaves me with one big question: If death is a fall, how in the world do we properly brace ourselves for it?

A CHANGE IN MINDSET:
*EM*BRACING OUR HARDEST FALL

I want to challenge the way we look at bracing for death. Very few people enjoy talking about end-of-life issues. In fact, according to Statista.com, over half of Americans have some fear of death.[64] It's no wonder that we seldom want to discuss the matter, let alone plan for it. If you are like most people, you are very uncomfortable thinking about your leaving of this earth. Because of that, you might have avoided preparing your family, your kids, and your business for your untimely departure.

As Christians, our attitude toward death should be different from the attitude of those who don't know Jesus. After all, we know that death is not the end! We know that, as Billy Graham once said, "The moment we take our last breath on earth, we take our first in heaven." [65] Because of that, we don't have to fear death. Instead, we *em*brace our homegoing. Believing God's promise of eternal life enables us to live by faith rather than fear and boldly take the proper steps to make sure that our homes and businesses are in good order when the Lord decides to bring us home.

I say all of this because I want you not only to read this chapter, but to be invested in making the legal preparations necessary to protect your kids, your family, and your business from undue hardship, stress, and further grief in your absence. In my humble opinion, this chapter has the single most important objective of this book. In fact, the subject of this chapter was the spark that triggered the idea of CapitalMoms in 2020!

PLAN FOR THE BEST AND PREPARE FOR THE WORST

Back in 2020, my friend and I were discussing the possibility of me caring for her children (my godchildren) in the event of her untimely death. At that point, I told her that she needed a will naming me as guardian. Sounds simple enough, right? Well, it was in my mind until my lovely business partner reminded me that my friend's children have a father, who has rights.

"Oh, that guy," I thought. Shai reminded me that he would have rights to his children unless he was dead or those rights were terminated.

How I truly felt about that is for a different book.

A few months later, my same friend and I were talking about her real estate investment properties. By the way, she is blessed with a full-time job teaching, she's a realtor, and she's a real estate investor, all while being a single mother. If this doesn't inspire you, I don't know what will!

Anyway, as we were discussing her investment properties, she told me how she would like her properties to pass to her children. But there was a problem with that. Her babies were both under ten years old. I said to her, "Friend, you can't leave whole property to minors. If you do, it may require a trustee to manage the property. That's assuming you have someone in mind whom you trust to manage it for however many years the children are not of adult age. At that point, the trustee will be entitled to pay for their management, and they might sell the property."

Being the bearer of bad news was not fun, but it prepared both of us to dive into these issues.

WILL YOU PLAN FOR YOUR CHILDREN?

I have yet to meet a mom who doesn't worry or at least think about what would happen to her children if she were to die before her kids reached adulthood, yet very few moms take proactive steps to assuage those worries! Please listen to me: estate planning is the most important step a CapitalMom can take to ensure that her children and her property are taken care of in the event of her untimely death. This looks different for different moms. Though there are many actions that can be taken and documents that can be drafted to conduct estate planning, the most familiar form of estate planning is a will.

According to Caring.com, despite increased awareness of death among Americans as a result of the worldwide pandemic, only a third of American adults have a will.[66] Interestingly, there has been an uptick among young adults when it comes to making plans for after their death, while there's been a downward trend among adults over fifty years of age. It's vital that we *all* understand the value of having a plan in place—the sooner, the better.

In biblical times, daughters didn't have an inheritance unless there were no sons alive when both parents passed away. Widows had it especially hard because the husbands were the breadwinners, so it was very difficult for these women to have a means of support. We see this illustrated in 2 Kings 4:1–7, which tells the story of the widow who was left with little to nothing after her husband's death. Are you ready for another Ebony version of Scripture from the Holy Bible?

One day, three men banged on the door of a recent widow. Startled by the noise, she walked slowly to the door while wiping away her tears. Her two young sons, one on each side, were gripping her garment and walking with her, slowing her down. When she answered the door, the men identified themselves as creditors.

"Your husband owes us talents! Where is he?" one creditor yelled belligerently.

She responded, sobbing, "He died three days ago, and I

have no way to pay you."

Another creditor snarled, "That sounds like a personal problem. Either you come up with the money before the next Sabbath, or we'll take your children as our slaves!"

The woman slams the door and cries for three straight days, only getting up to try to feed her boys.

The day before the Sabbath, the prophet Elisha came to visit, and she recognized him as a someone whom her husband worked for. "Your servant, my husband, is dead!" she said. "He was a good man and loved the Lord. But now he's gone, and creditors are coming to take our sons away as slaves!"

Elisha gasped audibly. He asked for some water while he thought. Elisha learned that this widow had only one jar of oil in the entire home, so he instructed her to get jars from all of her neighbors. The widow and her two boys ran around the cul-de-sac and asked to borrow everyone's empty jars.

Then the woman and her sons went back into their house, and she shut the door behind them, just as the prophet had told her to do. She started filling the jars, one by one, with oil. The small jar of oil she started with filled every single empty jar. The oil didn't stop until the last jar was filled.

The widow immediately sold the oil and used the profits to pay her husband's debt. And that's the story of how this widow was anointed and christened a CapitalMom. I'm just saying.

In our world today, women aren't normally left as the poor widow in the story. We women are the most educated demographic. The earning gap, although still prevalent, is decreasing as each year passes. I've met quite a few househusbands who don't bat an eye at their wives providing the money for the household while they take care of the home and children.

I say all of this because now, more than ever, CapitalMoms need to invest in estate planning. We need to make sure that our children will have proper guardians, our businesses can outlive us, our properties are managed, and our hard-earned assets go to the people and organizations of our choice.

For example, in Texas, if you have no will, the following general principles may apply upon your death:

- If you die married, your assets will go to your spouse.

- If you die unmarried, your assets will go to your children in equal shares.

- If you die single and without any living children, your assets will go to your grandchildren.

- If you die single without any descendants, your assets will go to your parents.

- If your parents are also deceased, your assets will go to your siblings in equal shares.

- If you die without any parents or siblings, your assets could go to your nieces and nephews.

- If you die without any known family members, your assets could go to the state!

It can get truly complicated if you have a blended family or half-siblings.

For some of us, this works out well, but for many, it's not that simple. That's where estate planning can assist:

- If you have children at different maturity levels or with different money management skills, you may want them to have different shares of your assets or different assets altogether.

- If you have a husband who is not the father of your children, you may want to ensure that your children are given certain assets.

- If you have an estranged sibling who took your spouse and moved halfway across the world, you may not want to give your assets to her.

- If you don't want your family or friends to have to go through probate, or court proceedings, in order to have your assets, great estate planning may assist with that as well.

The list could go on, but whatever your reason, you should ensure that your estate plan considers your circumstances and properly distributes your assets in the event of your death.

GUARDIANSHIP: WHOM WILL YOU *TRUST*?

Odds are that if you're reading this text, you are a mother and you want your assets to pass to your (adult) children or to be used to care for your (minor) children. Well, you should brace yourself for this news, lovely: legally, you cannot pass a significant amount of property to children who are minors.

Depending on how many assets and how much money you expect to have at the time of your death, you may want to create a trust, managed by a trustee, to care for your children. You can choose to have what's called a Guardian of the Person (the person who is responsible for the care of your children) and a Guardian of the Property or a trustee (the person who manages the money that takes care of your children and ensures that the balance is given to them as adults or at the specified time according to your will or trust). Often the same person manages the children and the children's property. In many instances, the parents don't have funds in an account to take care of the children.

Now, you may have insurance and think that should be enough to care for your children. But do you *trust* all your family members to take care of your children and the money? Do you trust them to use the money only for your children and not for themselves?

There's more protection in having two separate individuals involved in your estate who can act as checks and balances for one another, each ensuring that the other is doing the right thing by your children and in accordance with your wishes. However, the court can also monitor your estate with the correct wording in your will and/or trust.

It's also worth noting that you can create a trust for your pet, your favorite non-profit, or even your business. You can put assets like money or even a home in a trust. The options are truly lengthy, too much so for this book! You should discuss the possibility of a trust with a *trusted* estate planning attorney (puns are always intended around here) to determine what's best for you.

LONG-TERM ESTATE PLANNING: WHO GETS AND DOES WHAT?

I won't take long on this subject, but I normally advise our estate planning clients that long-term estate planning gets more complex over time. In other words, you may have two children under five years of age when you start your estate planning, but circumstances and relationships can change over time. I believe that it's a good idea to set a calendar reminder at least once every two years to review who your guardians are as well as who gets what. The couple you planned to care for your children may divorce, or you could learn that your values don't actually line up.

As your children get older, you may find that your son is a much better manager of money than your daughter is, although he is younger. In that case, you may want to name him trustee of money for your daughter. You may find that you have a child who is extremely co-dependent, or even disabled. Or you may have a child who is in school a lot longer than the other child, and you wish to assist that child through school if you pass away before he or she finishes. All these situations are reasons to update your estate plan.

Disinheritance

This may not even be on your radar, but what do you do when you don't want to give a family member *anything*?

Yes, that's a thing. Many people disinherit family members. I've personally written several wills that disinherited family members for one reason or another. I remember drafting a will for a soldier who disinherited his son because his son refused to speak to him. I've also drafted wills for a couple who disinherited a sister because of their strained relationship. I remember a mother who disinherited one of her daughters to whom she believed she had given enough during her lifetime.

Whatever your reason may be, you may choose to disinherit a family member, but keep in mind that a court will not likely allow a parent to completely disinherit a minor child whom the parent is financially responsible for supporting.

Administrator/Executor

An administrator or executor is the person responsible for ensuring that your wishes listed in your will come to fruition. This person should have great management and communication skills and be extremely trustworthy. Having an administrator is a fundamental part of managing your will as well as paying off debts and so forth. If you elect to name this person "independent," he or she won't have to be monitored by the court as much as a "dependent administrator" would be.

If the court must appoint an administrator, this person will likely be a dependent administrator, which means that he or she will have to post bond and report to the court periodically while your estate is settled.

When you name an administrator, you should also name a backup just in case.

As you can see, all these different ways to plan and prepare to ensure that your children, property, and assets will be taken care of the way you want upon your death are very significant and meaningful decisions. As with most other extraordinary decisions, I strongly recommend prayer and fasting for believers.

I've brought up fasting quite a bit in this book. Let's take a quick break from the legal jargon to dive deeper into fasting.

BIBLICAL FASTING: A DIVINE TOOL

Fasting is the privilege of abstaining from food. However, many of us use it synonymously with abstaining from anything important or meaningful in our lives to draw nearer to God. Coupled with prayer, fasting is something I often do when I'm going through a challenging time in my life, need to make important decisions, or want a deeper walk with the Lord. In fact, Shai and I have prayed and fasted about our writing of this book and for you as a reader, mother, and entrepreneur!

In relation to this chapter, prayer and fasting is a means to seek the Lord's direction, guidance, and *will* when it comes to your estate planning, including guardianship decisions.

People observe different types of fasts. As you review the different types, ask yourself which one stands out to you the most. What appeals to your health, lifestyle, and practicality? Consider these options:

- The total, complete, absolute fast is when you go without food and drink for an extended period (see Esther 4:16 for an example). Please note that it's dangerous to do this kind of fast for more than three days at a time.

- The most common fast is one that allows only drinking water. On this fast, you can normally go more than three days due to the hydration. It is believed that Jesus' famous forty-day fast was fasting from food and having only water (Luke 4:1–13).

- Another popular fast is called *intermittent fasting*, which is when you go without food and drink for certain time periods of the day.

- A *partial* fast is when you don't partake in certain foods and/or meals. Many observe Daniel's diet (see Daniel 10:2–3) as a fast. I once heard a pastor point out that Daniel wasn't fasting; he was simply refusing to eat the king's meat, according to his people's dietary rules. On that note, Daniel's diet wouldn't be a fast for people who already follow a vegetarian or vegan lifestyle of not eating meat. Regardless, if you hear the term *Daniel fast*, it means eating only fruits, vegetables, and legumes and drinking water or 100 percent juices.

- Some partake in a *sacrifice* and call it a fast. A sacrifice could be to abstain from sex (through mutual agreement if a married couple; see 1 Corinthians 7:5), social media, television, entertainment, or hobbies. No matter what it is, it should actually be a sacrifice for you and free up time for you to spend with God.

Deciding what to fast from is totally up to you. I normally feel led regarding why and how to fast, but that is certainly not a requirement. Remember that God looks at the heart! I make a point not to fast with the desire to lose weight. As I said, God knows our hearts, so I'm certain that He would be able to see through my false motives.

When fasting, I like to read the Word and pray when I would otherwise be eating or partaking in what I am abstaining from. I personally try to fast often, especially when I need to make big, non-obvious decisions and want to hear from my Father. For example, my husband and I fasted while dating and prior to marrying. Shai and I fasted prior to becoming business partners, and we still fast the first of each month. I fast for the sick, I fast for those hurting, I fast for my friends, and I fast for my children. I recently took up fasting for my family members on their birthdays.

The point of the matter is that fasting is a privilege and a divine tool we are all equipped with to help us tap into communication with God. Fasting coupled with prayer is a great way to ensure that your decisions are divinely inspired.

Now back to the legal-schmegal.

PREPARING FOR THE UNEXPECTED

Estate planning is more than a will and/or trust pertaining to your death. It also plans for times in your life when you could become incapacitated or no longer able to make rational decisions for yourself. In these cases, you may want to consider the following documents as well:

- *Advance Directive* lets medical professionals know when you would like to be put on life-sustaining assistance.

- *Medical Power of Attorney* allows another individual (agent) to make medical decisions for you in an emergency or when you would otherwise not be able to do so on your own.

- *Other Power of Attorney* designates an agent as responsible for paying your (the principal's) bills or performing other actions while you're still living but unable to do those things on your own.

Keep in mind that these documents only last while you are alive. While I was in the Army, I once visited a client at her home. She was an Army Sergeant First Class (SFC, E-7) dying of cancer. She needed a power of attorney for her adult son to pay her bills. I remember her being so weak that she couldn't speak and had to be fed. Her family was doing their best just to keep her comfortable. I had to help her sign the paperwork and respond to my questions with simple head nods.

After she passed, her son attempted to use the power of attorney that was installed for her living decisions to access her account, but it doesn't work that way. Powers of attorney expire on the expiration date listed or at the death of the principal. When she passed, so did the power of attorney.

If there isn't a legal will or named beneficiary, a representative may have to go to court and be named the administrator. I say "may" because, depending on your state and the amount of assets, there are ways to avoid probate. *Probate* is the process that involves the court ensuring the proper distribution of a deceased person's assets. You probate a will, or you may go through the probate process if someone dies without a will.

Four of the most common ways to avoid having to go to probate court are:

1. naming a beneficiary on your retirement savings, stocks, bonds, and the like;

2. naming a joint owner or successor on your bank account;

3. naming a joint owner on your real and personal property (such as your vehicle titles); and

4. having an Enhanced Life Estate Deed (sometimes referred to as a Lady Bird Deed or a Quitclaim Deed) naming a beneficiary to take ownership immediately upon your death.

The benefit of taking these measures is that your relatives can avoid probate, as would have been the case for the adult son previously mentioned. However, these options can be very costly if you don't get it right the first time. We advise you to discuss each option and its pros and cons with a trusted estate planning attorney.

THERE'S MORE TO DEATH THAN PASSING DOWN ASSETS

Have you planned your funeral? My guess is probably not. I don't blame you; it's all a little creepy. But it's totally healthy and helpful to plan your funeral for the benefit of the loved ones you leave behind. Your family will likely be in such a difficult place that they won't enjoy picking out a casket, a plot of land, or an outfit for you to be buried in. They won't want to argue over the right earrings to bury with you.

I once had a client who needed a will as her last step in completing her estate planning. She was single with only one adult daughter. She told me that her daughter was extremely emotional and she did not trust that her daughter could control her emotions to the degree that would be required to handle the details of her death and burial. For that reason, she had already purchased her casket and her plot of land and had all her documents organized and ready for someone else to serve as the administrator or executor (depending on the state). I commend her for knowing her child and conducting herself accordingly. It's one thing to know your child; it's a whole other thing to use that knowledge to prepare fully for your death.

STORING YOUR ESTATE PLAN

There is no certain place you are required or expected to keep your estate planning documents, but you should put them where your administrator or executor can find them. Also, though it depends on whom you consult with regarding your estate plan, I am not a fan of having copies of your plan. Copies can be probated in Texas, and who is to say that they will find the latest version of your will if you keep copies of them? You would have to ensure that all copies are destroyed once you execute another will.

And here is a little extra nugget of advice for you. When my husband and I prepared our first will years ago, we were told that we could put our wills in freezer bags inside of the freezer. That way, they would be less likely to be destroyed in a fire or flood, and unlike a safe deposit box, no one would need a court order to access them. Equally important, you should keep your passwords, keys, and anything else that would affect your administrator's ability to manage your affairs in a safe place that, again, your administrator can access.

Keeping Your Estate Plan Up-to-Date

We can rest assured that circumstances will inevitably change at various stages of our lives. Your children will get older, you may marry, your spouse may die, you may divorce, and you will have a different amount of assets, whether greater or less.

Because changing circumstances are certain, you should review your plan at least once every five years or if:

- You open a new bank account.

- You purchase real estate.

- You marry.

- You divorce.

- You make a major investment.

- You open a business.

- You develop a terminal illness.

- A beneficiary passes away.

- A guardian passes away.

- You have more children or adopt.

Basically, if there is any major change in your life, you should revisit your estate plan. Notice that the common thread in the list above is that there are major liability implications with these events, so you should be mindful of ensuring that your plan accurately reflects your wishes.

DO YOU NEED A BUSINESS SUCCESSION PLAN?

Do you have a plan for your business in the event of your untimely death, illness, or retirement? You may not have one. Moreover, you may not need one. A business succession plan names who will do what in order to keep your business running successfully.

If you're anything like me, you do the job of fifteen people and would find it difficult to find just one person to do everything you do. If that's the case, your succession plan can include multiple individuals who will have different responsibilities, with the intent to carry on the business years after you're gone.

Without a succession plan for a company that has multiple employees, processes and knowledge could be lost, the business culture could be negatively impacted, and the business could fail.

There are several online resources to help you start a business succession plan, but to get started, you can:

- Write down all the tasks you personally ensure are completed and that must be done to make your business run smoothly.

- Include whom you want to do it (and have a backup plan if they can't or won't).

- Create the training or information needed to empower the successor. You may also list certain language in your company/operating agreement that states who gets your shares in the event of your death, which could function as a will of sorts. (But *please* get an attorney involved!)

If you have a business partner, you may consider life insurance for yourself with your business partner listed as the beneficiary as part of your estate plan. This is extremely considerate and sets your partner up for success in the event of your untimely death. Just like your assets, your business should be left in good hands.

If you're a sole proprietor or a single-member LLC, the company will likely die with you if you fail to plan. If you're okay with that, a business succession plan may be unnecessary. But if you want to build an empire, you had better make a plan!

WHAT HAPPENS TO A BUSINESS IF ONE OF THE BUSINESS OWNERS GETS A DIVORCE?

I feel terrible writing so much about death, divorce, and illness in this chapter, but I sure hope that it helps you to feel more prepared in the event of a *fall*!

Many business owners don't think about how their partner's divorce could affect their business. Depending on what state you're residing in, your business could be considered *community property*. Community property is property acquired during marriage that belongs to both spouses no matter who initially acquired the property or formed the business.

For instance, imagine that you've founded an extremely

successful company that teaches women how to write software, and your employees train hundreds of women each year. You gross $100 million in a year. What happens if you and your husband divorce? He may legally be entitled to half of what your company is worth!

It's worth noting that a great way to address business ownership in marriage is by having your spouse sign your *properly* drafted company/operating agreement. (We talked about this in the January chapter.) Your agreement can have language that specifies what the parties agree to in the event that they divorce. It would serve as a kind of postnuptial agreement, but just for business interests.

MANAGING EXPECTATIONS

Although there are a great number of conflicts recorded in the Bible, I believe that God wants us to avoid conflict wherever we can by showing His love, patience, and kindness. Therefore, as we thoughtfully prepare for our family to take our assets, we should manage expectations as much as possible to prevent unnecessary conflict between our family members upon our earthly exit.

How you express your desires can be the difference between a family completely breaking down and a family coming together. You should prioritize informing your family and friends of your expectations regarding administration, guardianship, and how your assets will be divided. You can communicate this in a number of ways, but here are some ideas for how you can manage the expectations of your family members and friends:

- Have a phone call with everyone listed in your estate plan, letting them know what decisions you've made, and ensure that the administrator agrees to manage your assets.

- Have a family meeting to discuss your estate plan and expectations of everyone.

- Write personalized letters to accompany your estate plan that express your love and the thoughtful consideration that went into making your decisions.

- Video record yourself sharing your fondest memories and expressing why you made the decisions you made with your estate plan. (This is my personal favorite.)

You can even do a combination of all these ideas! What's most important is that you prepare your loved ones so there is mutual understanding and, hopefully, less conflict.

I once had a client who had two daughters, but he planned to leave everything to just one of them. At first glance, it may appear that he hated his one daughter and was being cruel, yet that wasn't the case at all. He loved both of his daughters but felt as if he had already given one of them her inheritance *during* his lifetime. Therefore, it was important to him that his other daughter, who never requested or needed her dad's money during his lifetime, would have her fair share after his death.

It was a perfectly reasonable thing to do, but in my

humble opinion, required an explanation for his daughters to avoid any fighting when he died. For that reason, I advised the client to make some adjustments, primarily not to disinherit one of his daughters completely but instead to list things he planned to give her beforehand. I also recommended that he have the discussion with his daughters *now* to help avoid fighting between the sisters *later*.

IT'S DUE SEASON!

Some things in life we simply cannot avoid, and this chapter has gone into detail about the most important thing you need to confront and plan for: your ascension to heaven! By *em*bracing the fall, you can make the lives of the ones you love easier. Completing your estate plan, keeping it up to date, having a business succession plan, and responsibly deciding who will have and do what are great ways to comfort your family during the most upsetting of times.

This month, take the time to communicate your wishes to your loved ones. My favorite way to do this is to record a video for each child, for the guardian, and for your administrator. Even if you don't have a will, recording a video and letting your loved ones know what you want is a great way to get started with your estate plan.

Consider avoiding solemn language like "death" and using more hopeful language instead. Here's an example: "I'm leaving you this video to tell you how much Mommy loves you and why I wanted you to have my father's fishing line."

No matter how you choose to communicate your wishes

and intentions, don't forget to make your estate plan legally sufficient by contacting an attorney. While we're at it, let's just go ahead and schedule that consultation within the next thirty days. Write your consultation date and time here:

_____.

September Notes

October:
Scare Tactics —
When the Enemy Says, "Boo"

Shinia Lambert

Scared is what we're feeling but brave is what we're doing.[67]

—Emma Donoghue

Fear [noun]: an unpleasant emotion caused by the belief that someone or something is dangerous, likely to cause pain, or a threat.[68]

In this chapter, I hope to help you identify common fears associated with starting a business and teach you how to overcome any self-sabotaging dialogue that may cause you to doubt your calling or inhibit your personal and business success.

To set the tone, let's start off with a powerful quote by

Priscilla Shirer. In her book *Fervent*, she wrote, "If I were your enemy, I'd magnify your fears, making them appear insurmountable, intimidating you with enough worries until avoiding them becomes your driving motivation. I would use anxiety to cripple you, to paralyze you, leaving you indecisive, clinging to safety and sameness, always on the defensive because of what might happen. When you hear the word faith, all I'd want you to hear is 'unnecessary risk'." [69]

Wow.

Please read the last line from that quote again. Can you relate to that? I sure can.

Prior to reading that quote, have you ever thought of making your faith synonymous with unnecessary risk? I certainly hadn't!

I must admit that I wasn't afraid when I made the decision in 2018 to go into business for myself. Why not? There are three main reasons. First, I was overcome with excitement about the thrill of something new, the hope of a fresh start, and the clout of having my name on the marquee outside of our office suites. Second, I was partnering with a woman I loved, admired, and trusted, so it didn't feel nearly as terrifying as it would have been had I been going it alone.

Last and probably most importantly, I felt like I had plenty of time. For the past several years, I'd been practicing family law as an Assistant Attorney General with the Office of the Attorney General Child Support Division, and I wasn't planning on resigning until the fall of 2019. Sure, I was up for a promotion that would guarantee me six figures and had great benefits (while being a single mom with a mortgage), but I wasn't worried, because it was still all talk. I had plenty of time—until the Lord gave me a resignation date: May 2019.

Wait, that wasn't what I'd been planning. I wanted one last statewide conference with my team. I wanted to be able to put some more money away. I wanted to, I don't know, lose a little weight first. Pick out the right office furniture. Pray about it again. I just needed more time.

As it turns out, that's where I'd placed my faith, in the time delay. When God took away my security blanket, my fear was revealed. Deep down, I *was* afraid. I was afraid of failing. I was afraid that as a single mother of a son (of whom I am pretty fond) that I wouldn't be able to continue to provide the lifestyle we had become accustomed to. I was afraid of letting my new partner down. I was afraid of disappointing my parents, Wanda and Darren. I was afraid of what people would say or think and of what they would *not* say.

The enemy was having a field day with me. What had begun as this joyous, life-altering faith leap had morphed into this stressful, life-altering fear flop. I was afraid, and I didn't want to admit it. How could I, in one breath, proclaim that I was doing what God called me to do and, in the next, be too afraid to walk it out?

Easily. Because I'm human, and so are you.

I'm proud to say—and, hopefully, you've discerned—that I didn't let my fears get in the way of my purpose. What is more important than knowing that I overcame my fears is believing that you can, too. You are not alone.

I recently polled a group of intelligent, creative, and driven entrepreneurs about their greatest fears when going into business. As I reviewed the responses, I was overwhelmed with a common theme: not one prospective or current business owner questioned their gift, their talent, or the quality of the product or service they provide. Every fear was centered on how that gift, talent, product, or service would be received, such as: *"What if no one follows my social media?" "What if no one purchases my product?" "What if no one values my service?"* Ultimately, these fears culminated in a bigger one: *"What will I do if I fail?"*

Failure is a very real and valid concern. After all, even the Bible admonishes us to consider the cost before beginning a project. Who would be foolish enough to begin a business without considering all the possible outcomes? We certainly aren't suggesting that you ignore red flags and jump into entrepreneurship blindly, but we also aren't encouraging you to delay your destiny by finding reasons why it won't work.

Let's remember that we are not just physical beings; we are also emotional, mental, and spiritual beings. So, if we are talking about approaching business from a healthy and confident place, we must address the internal conversations that we are having with ourselves. What internal dialogue do you have on repeat? Is it helping to contribute to your success or sending you into a tailspin of failure?

FEAR OF CHALLENGES AND THE UNKNOWN

Self-sabotaging internal dialogue: "I've never done this before. There's no way God could be calling me to do this. Even if I were interested, this is too much, too fast, and too soon. I mean, why would anyone care what I have to say, want to buy my product, or hire me for my services?"

If we are not careful, we will self-protect (a nice way of saying sabotage) our way right out of our blessing. Challenges or obstacles are not synonymous with failure. Starting a business is difficult. There's no way around that. There are parts that can be simplified, especially with the right tools and knowledge. Much of it can be exhilarating and enjoyable. But make no mistake: starting, maintaining, and growing a business is an enormous amount of hard work. That doesn't mean it's not worth it!

When challenges and obstacles come—when you're faced with something you've never done before, when you're presented with an opportunity to rely more on God than on your gifts, when you feel overwhelmed with the pace you're expected to keep—embrace it! On the other side of that challenge or obstacle is the very thing you need to take your business to the next level. Greater knowledge and experience are on the other side of that challenge. Greater passion and deeper compassion are on the other side of the obstacle. More opportunities, greater exposure, your next big breakthrough—it's all on the other side of right now. This moment is all you have.

Read this Scripture passage from Luke 1:26–33 (NLT):

In the sixth month of Elizabeth's pregnancy, God sent the angel Gabriel to Nazareth, a village in Galilee, to a virgin named Mary. She was engaged to be married to a man named Joseph, a descendant of King David. Gabriel appeared to her and said, "Greetings, favored woman! The Lord is with you!"

Confused and disturbed, Mary tried to think what the angel could mean. "Don't be afraid, Mary," the angel told her, "for you have found favor with God! You will conceive and give birth to a son, and you will name him Jesus. He will be very great and will be called the Son of the Most High. The Lord God will give him the throne of his ancestor David. And he will reign over Israel forever; his Kingdom will never end!"

I want you to imagine a young girl approximately fourteen to fifteen years of age, because that's how old Mary would have been when we encounter the mother of Jesus for the first time in the Bible. Now imagine the unprecedented occurrence of an angel appearing to this girl. Just take that in for a moment. This was burning-bush big. This didn't happen every day. God had been silent for four hundred years, and then an angel appeared and essentially said to Mary (who was a teenager, a virgin, and engaged to be married), "You're going to give birth to a child—God's child! Surprise, Mary! You are greatly favored!"

"What?" I can imagine her thinking.

She was experiencing something that had never been and would never be experienced by another human being on this planet. How was she supposed to tell Joseph, her fiancé? How was she supposed to tell her family? How do you explain something like that? How quickly was the rumor mill going to start spinning? Her integrity would be questioned, and her purity would be doubted—all at the most inconvenient time of her life.

"I'm favored?" I can imagine her thinking.

She could have been ostracized, cast out, and disowned. At the same time, she was being asked to believe God for what seemed, by any standard, to be impossible. Not perceived as hard. Not tough. Not difficult. A child born of a virgin? Impossible.

Of all the things it might have felt like, I guarantee you that it didn't feel like favor. Maybe a trial. A dark season. A valley experience. A judgment.

We can call it unfair.

God calls it favor.

A Few Words About God's Favor

Okay, I may be dating myself here, but do you remember an MTV documentary series from back in 2000 that opened with, "You think you know ... but you have no idea"? Then the episode would be "the Diary of" a celebrity, such as Jennifer Lopez or Alicia Keys.

The premise of the show *Diary* was that whether it was the result of popular opinion, rumors, or common knowledge, there was something that everyone thought they understood about someone, but—*aha!*—they were wrong.

What if I were to tell you that it's possible for us to think that we know something to be true about God's Word that isn't, or at least not exactly. I want to propose to you that we may be misunderstanding what it means to be favored by God. And in this season when we are passionately pursuing growth and making deliberate decisions that affect the course and direction of our lives, we cannot afford to get God's favor wrong.

If you've been favored—and you have—then you've been entrusted with something that God not only expects you to do, but is depending on you to do. Favor is equipping. Favor is the entryway into your calling. Favor means that God has positioned you to carry out His plans for your life.

God's favor doesn't mean that it's going to be easy or that it's always going to be enjoyable. It certainly doesn't mean that it's going to be convenient. If we don't get our understanding of favor right, we'll start to think of favor as a curse. We'll start to think of favor as a trial.

But favor is neither of those things. Favor is what's getting us through the trial and to the blessing. Favor is what enables us to stand when our legs want to give way. Favor is what keeps us hoping when our circumstances say that we should give up. Favor prioritizes truth over facts.

Noah was favored by God, but Noah had a task ahead of him that was unheard of. He was a man who had to build an ark but had no idea what an ark was! He had to build something he'd never seen in preparation for something he'd never experienced. Until the time of the flood, it had never rained; the earth was watered from underneath. Stay with me. God's favor looks like putting us in a situation to do something we've never done so we can experience something we've never experienced.

Mary did something that had never been done and experienced something she'd otherwise never have experienced. Dare we mention Jesus? The Ultimate One did what had never been done and could never have been accomplished by anyone else so that we could experience what could not otherwise have ever been experienced: eternal life, reconciliation with God, and lives filled with purpose.

Woman of God, CapitalMom, you are greatly favored. This is your time.

The most important opportunities of your life rarely present themselves when they are convenient.

We can call it unfair.

Don't be afraid.

God still calls it favor.

Faith Over Fear

God's love for you is not shown by the ease of your life, but by the protection and provision He gives you through every season. Think about it. If there were no danger, why would you need protection? If there were no lack in any area, why would you need provision?

To make your idea of success dependent upon ease is to short-change yourself of the very growth and opportunities for faith that you were created for. Instead of replaying the old dialogue that tells you that something new or challenging is scary and intimidating, try creating a new dialogue that embraces whatever lies ahead, whether you perceive it to be enjoyable or uncomfortable.

Your new internal dialogue to combat the fear of challenges and the unknown is this: "I don't have to fear the challenges of stepping into the unknown, because God is always with me. He has promised that He will strengthen, help, and hold me with His 'victorious right hand'" (Isaiah 41:10 NLT).

Ask yourself this: In whose hands will God place the most important tasks, the faithful or the fearful?

FEAR OF OTHER PEOPLE'S OPINIONS

Self-sabotaging internal dialogue: "Ninety percent of businesses fail. Who am I to think that my business will be any different? Doesn't starting a business mean that I need a college or graduate degree, lots of money, and an expensive attorney?"

This fear is dangerous because it combines your insecurities with the voices of those you presented your ideas to who instead of encouraging you, presented you with a list of questions. Have you noticed that? Most naysayers don't speak facts; they ask questions. That's because those who are most discouraging are typically people who have not accomplished something themselves and, therefore, cannot speak definitively on anything. Instead, they aim to discourage you from accomplishing your dreams.

While we will all encounter individuals like these, for the most part, a certain level of maturity allows you to discard the opinions of people who clearly don't have your best interest at heart. If you take nothing else from this section, remember that it is unwise to share your vision with everyone. Being careful about whom you share your vision with will protect both your vision and your faith in it.

When you share something as precious as your vision with a person you are not called to share it with, you risk allowing that individual's doubts or disbelief to dilute your vision into something "manageable," something that's easily believable and less risky. Furthermore, you potentially open yourself up to fears that hadn't even entered your mind. Now you find yourself doubting if you even heard from God at all. You end up asking yourself, *"Why in the world did I think that I could do this in the first place?"* It's a slippery slope, isn't it?

There's clearly a time to disregard and discard the opinions of others, but is it ever appropriate to consider what others have to say about your business venture? You don't want to let other people's opinions distract you from being who you're called to be and doing what you're called to do. On the other hand, if you're human, you're likely engaged in some relationships as you embark on this journey to becoming a business owner. You may be a spouse, a parent, a friend, a sibling, someone's beloved child, a leader, a mentor, and so forth. Those relationships require time, commitment, responsibility, sacrifice, and attention. Those relationships will continue to require these things of you even after you declare to the world your intention to make it big in business. As a result, it would be wise to consider the opinions and counsel of those you do life with.

The Bible tells us plainly that seeking counsel is wise:

- "The way of a fool is right in his own eyes, but a wise man listens to advice" (Proverbs 12:15 ESV).

- "Where there is no guidance, a people falls, but in an abundance of counselors there is safety" (Proverbs 11:14 ESV).

- "Without counsel plans fail, but with many advisers they succeed" (Proverbs 15:22 ESV).

There's nothing inherently wrong with asking others for their opinion or advice or with considering how your next important business decision might affect those who love and depend on you. Instead of completely discarding the idea that other people's opinions matter, maybe ask yourself *why* they matter. We want to be mindful that we don't start to crave the affirmation of others and let our decisions rise and fall on another's approval of us.

Picture a quarterback in the middle of the Super Bowl. In a critical play, right before the ball is snapped, imagine him calling a timeout, jogging to the stands, and discussing the next play with a spectator. The quarterback listens intently while the spectator opines. Finally satisfied that he's gotten the approval of the spectator, the quarterback heads back to the field to resume play.

Now picture Oprah Winfrey before she's about to sign a multi-million-dollar contract for a new venture. Imagine her pausing and asking her administrative assistant, "Do you think this is a good idea?" Oprah listens intently to the administrative assistant's opinion. Satisfied that she's gotten her approval, Oprah signs the contract.

With these two playful hypotheticals, I'm trying to illustrate that not everyone around you is meant to play a significant role in your entrepreneurial pursuit and decisions. Some people can be spectators or assistants, and that's okay. It certainly doesn't devalue them as people, but it should heighten your awareness that not every opinion ought to be weighed the same.

Your new internal dialogue to replace the fear of other people's opinions is this: "I don't fear other people's opinions, because while everyone has value, not everyone contributes value to me. At the end of the day, I will trust in the Lord. He is where I ultimately find my confidence." Proverbs 29:25 reads, "Fearing people is a dangerous trap, but trusting the LORD means safety" (NLT).

Stop putting so much weight on what other people think about what you're being called to do. If God wanted them in your game, He would have put them on the field and not on the sidelines.

FEAR OF SACRIFICING ALL

Self-sabotaging internal dialogue: "If I want to succeed in business, I need to forsake everyone and everything else. Nothing else matters. Blood. Sweat. Tears. Early mornings and late nights. It's got to be all or nothing."

I recall a time when Ebony was in my office celebrating the fact that she got to make her kids bacon for breakfast that morning, and I was ecstatic about being able to cook dinner that week for my son and sitting down to eat together. As two mothers, one happily married and one happily single, who are also managing attorneys of our own firm, we found joy in our life balance.

In that moment, we redefined what being an awesome mom and attorney looked like. But we also knew that the definition could change again the next week. We learned that we had the freedom to adjust, and we had to be okay with no two days being the same. We welcomed the fluidity. We embraced the unpredictable. By controlling what we could and making allowances for what we couldn't, we took the pressure off ourselves to be perfect. As a result, we got to be awesome partners and parents who were grateful for grace!

We lovingly managed the expectations of our families and kept in constant communication with our support systems to make sure that we didn't let our work commitments spill over into our precious and limited personal time at home. We understood that while, without a doubt, we were called to this firm, we had loved ones and responsibilities that had previously been entrusted to us. At no point did we believe that we had God's permission to forsake them.

Letting go of this fear means being okay with saying, "I'm not excelling in every area." It means being open to the different seasons of life and being okay with going through a drive-through for the second time this week. Sure, maybe we could meal prep more on the weekend, or maybe we could use that same time to engage with our kids. No judgment on the meal prepping, by the way, we are all for it. We found and, from day to day, continue to find what works for us. We encourage you to step outside of the tidy box of society's expectations and find what works for you and your family.

In a conversation among up-and-coming female entrepreneurs at a recent leadership conference,[70] we overhead one of the panelists mention something to the effect of, "I will forsake anyone and anything to never lose myself again." While I can understand the passion behind that statement, I can't agree with its content. If finding ourselves means forsaking others, I think that we've overestimated our complexity.

When left unchecked, fear can cause us to deny truth, discount giftedness, and defer our dreams. Let's replace that negative internal dialogue one more time!

Your new internal dialogue to combat the fear of sacrificing all is this: "I don't have to fear working myself to death or failing in other areas of my life while pursuing entrepreneurship. I know that 'I can do all things [I am called to and created for] through Christ who strengthens me,' like Philippians 4:13 says (NKJV)."

A successful entrepreneur can approach situations that may create fear and, rather than becoming fearful, can discern reasonable risks and confidently make decisions that further her business goals.

FEAR OF FAILURE

One of the most obvious and common fears associated with starting a business is that it won't be successful and will ultimately fail. In a day and age when we try to put a positive spin on everything, including failure, by using expressions like "failing forward," "every failure is a lesson learned," and "fail better," at the end of the day, things not working out the way you dreamed still hurts. Sorry, but it does.

Businesses do fail every day. I don't say that to discourage you, especially not after you've done all the work so far in this book, but because I believe that knowledge is power. I don't want you to go into business unaware. Did you know that businesses don't fail because of the product or service, lack of interest from customers, or even oversaturation in the marketplace? One of the number one reasons businesses fail is because the business owner gives up. Whether the owner becomes overwhelmed or burned out, is presented with another opportunity, or experiences a change in structure, rarely does a business fail because of the business in and of itself. Can your business fail? Yes. Can your business be bigger, better, and more impactful than you ever imagined? Also yes.

While I wouldn't equate any of the following terms with failure, a business can go through stages in which its existence or structure changes, and a lack of familiarity with these stages and changes can be anxiety-inducing for the owner(s). The following isn't meant to be an exhaustive canon or even terms that we expect you to wield daily. That said, did you know that to be an expert in an area, you really only need to know 10 percent more than the people in the room with you? Consider these legal nuggets that we've been giving you in each chapter *your* 10 percent!

Merger and Acquisition (M & A)

Definitions. A merger is when two businesses form a new legal entity under one name. An acquisition is when one business purchases another outright.[71]

Why a merger occurs. Generally, the idea behind a merger is that the interests in both businesses are merged into one. This presents an opportunity for a new entity, formed by the two businesses, which stands to make more money by reducing competition and risk.

Why an acquisition occurs. One company, which is generally larger than the other, agrees to purchase the smaller company. The larger company will then control the operations of the smaller company. Large companies acquire small businesses to grow, reduce competition, or to corner a niche in the marketplace.

Positive: A merger or acquisition can be a great means to grow your business or come underneath a business with greater resources, capital, and experience. An acquisition also means that most executives will keep their positions within the acquired company.

Conversion

Definition. A conversion takes place when a business decides that it wants to convert or change from one business entity type to another, effectively altering its legal structure, and register that change with its Secretary of State.

Why a conversion occurs. There are many reasons why an entrepreneur may decide to convert his or her business from one entity type to another. Most commonly, businesses elect to convert because there are advantages that they find attractive with another legal structure, such as the protection of a limited liability company. Others may find the need to garner financial support and want to convert to a corporation that can offer shares to potential investors. There are special requirements for a conversion to take place that may differ from state to state. If you are considering a conversion, it is highly recommended that you speak with a business law attorney. On a side note, registering your sole proprietorship with the state and electing a business entity type is not a conversion.

Positive. Conversions allow an entrepreneur to retain control over the legal structure of his or her business and to elect, when necessary, a structure that works best for that season of the business. Although repeated conversions are not recommended, it does provide some comfort to new business owners to know that they are not forever bound to their initial entity-type selection.

Dissolution

Definition. A dissolution is a process by which a business formally closes. When you formally close your business, you file articles of dissolution with the state, and as a result, the state no longer considers the business active.[72]

Why dissolution occurs. A business may dissolve because the business owner wants to end the business, the business is no longer lucrative, or the business owner has decided to move on to another business venture.

An involuntary dissolution can occur if the business is not complying with the requirements of the state in which it is registered. These requirements could include a failure to pay annual reports or taxes, failure to designate a registered agent, or mismanagement of the business.

Positive. A dissolution is positive if it's the move that you, as the business owner, want to make. You are in control, and a dissolution cannot occur unless you either (1) elect to dissolve your business or (2) fail to comply with the state's requirements.

As we close this chapter on fear, I hope that this brief exploration of these intimidating legal terms allows you to see that while going into business does contain risk, you have many options ahead of you to frame what you want your business to look like and opportunities to embrace changes that allow your vision to be fluid and expand.

IT'S DUE SEASON!

In 2021, during a virtual conference held by Tracy Litt, she spoke about how personal responsibility plays a huge role in fear because fear takes our power and makes it external to us. Fear tells us that our success is in someone else's hands. The following impactful activity, designed by Tracy, helps us to break down where the real power lies.

Take out a sheet of paper and make two columns. At the top of the left column, write, "What I Want." At the top of the right column, write, "Why I Don't Have It."

For example, when I took a shot at this exercise, I wrote in the left column, "I want more time to focus on my business pursuits."

After some reflection, I wrote in the right column, "I don't have this because I allow everyone else's needs to take priority over mine."

Once I acknowledged the reason why I didn't have what I truly wanted, I could start working on the changes I needed to make so that I *could* have it.

In my example, this might look like creating non-negotiable white space on my calendar for my business planning and keeping an appointment with myself the same way I would with a client. It's not just about prioritizing tasks; it's about prioritizing me. No more excuses. No more fear. That's power.

Now it's your turn.

On your piece of paper, jot down in the left column everything you desire to possess but are currently lacking. There is no right or wrong answer.

Now truly reflect on and be honest with yourself about *why* you don't have those things. As you do so, you'll find that what you desire is not only possible, but totally within your control.

Where is the power? Within!

October Notes

November:
In Thanksgiving—Exude Gratitude

Ebony Todd

I've learned that people will forget what you said, people will forget what you did, but people will never forget how you made them feel.[73]

—Maya Angelou

Thanksgiving [noun]: an open display of gratitude to God.

I love this definition of *thanksgiving* so much! It reminds me of how the word *thanks* and its derivatives are mentioned over one hundred times in the Bible! Here are some of my favorites that inspire gratefulness (emphasis is mine):

- "Do not be anxious about anything, but in every situation, by prayer and petition, with *thanksgiving*, present your requests to God" (Philippians 4:6 NIV).

- "Rejoice always, pray continually, give *thanks* in all

circumstances; for this is God's will for you in Christ Jesus" (1 Thessalonians 5:16–18 NIV).

- "So then, just as you received Christ Jesus as Lord, continue to live your lives in him, rooted and built up in him, strengthened in the faith as you were taught, and overflowing with *thankfulness*" (Colossians 2:6–7 NIV).

It's clear that God expects gratitude and thankfulness to be basic principles, morals, and values for us all.

LINKING GRATITUDE TO
TRUE BUSINESS SUCCESS

Thanksgiving as a principle in business is much more than simply saying "thank you" or having it prominently displayed on something you give to your customers.

I've been caught in a tennis match of meaningless expressions of gratitude before. I'm sure that the first time I said, "Thank you so much," I meant it, but by the fifth time, I was uncomfortable and only facetiously repeating the words with the hope of ending the match.

And who hasn't received to-go food from a local mom-and-pop restaurant in a bag labeled with a prominent "Thank You" in red while the grumpy individual giving it to you didn't even make eye contact, much less exude gratitude?

Colossians 3:15–17 reads, "And let the *peace* of Christ rule in your *hearts*, to which indeed you were called in one body. And be thankful. Let the word of Christ dwell in you richly, teaching and admonishing one another in all wisdom, *singing* psalms and hymns and spiritual songs, with thanksgiving in your *hearts* to God. And whatever you do, in word or deed, do everything in the name of the Lord Jesus, giving thanks to God the Father through him" (ESV, emphasis added).

Being thankful is not lip service. It's an attitude of appreciation, a spirit we exude. The scripture above references peace, hearts, and singing. It essentially describes gratitude as a certain level of peace in our hearts that enables us to sing, by instinct, a humble melody of thankfulness.

My mother often reminds me of a time, decades ago, when we were riding in the car together. My father was driving, my mother was in the passenger seat, and my younger sister and I were in the back seats. I was looking out of the rear window while my mother passionately disclosed her disdain for something of mine. I can't recall if it was my hair, outfit, or boyfriend, but it was something that bothered her that day. My response was a very simple, even-tempered but barbed "Thanks."

It may be difficult for you to imagine how I said, "Thanks," by reading the word, but it still resonates with my mother almost two decades later! It was a voluminous "Thanks." In that moment, my mother knew that I wasn't speaking graciously or with humility. She knew that I was upset with her and really wanted her to stop talking. Even though I said the word "thanks," my mother knew that I wasn't exuding gratitude but was being disrespectful.

Let's make one fact plain: I respected (and feared) my

mother enough to refrain from saying anything else!

What I learned from that experience is that true gratitude is evident and easy to identify regardless of the words you use. It's in the way you make someone feel.

Infusing your business with thanksgiving requires actions that are supported by genuine feelings of gratitude. It is a feeling you *have* as much as it is a feeling you *give* another person. It requires you to be in the moment when you're handing out your product and being present as you provide services.

Acting with a spirit of thanksgiving will not allow you to be sarcastic, demeaning, or hateful toward other people. It doesn't mean that you will never say or do something that someone else may not like or desire, but it does mean that you will speak and act from a peace-driven, content, and humble heart.

Beth Moore, the highly regarded minister, once wrote, "True humility is not low self-esteem ... humility is focused on God. Graciousness is true humility." [74]

On its face, thanking someone requires some level of humility. Arrogant people may not even say, "Thank you," because they believe that they can do everything on their own, without the assistance of others. Moreover, people who are constantly setting new goals or are, as my husband would say, "never satisfied" may find it difficult to appreciate what they already have and be content.

We should abstain from arrogance and should exercise contentment with our customers and clients alike. But let's get one thing straight: humility doesn't require insecurity or timidity. A true balance must be mastered between confidence in Christ and the talents bestowed on one side and graciousness and humility on the other. Mastering this balance is more likely to encourage clients and customers to work with a business owner even when the prices may be higher, or to travel further to patronize your business.

My business partner and I have expressed gratitude to our clients in several ways. For instance, our clients will receive an email thanking them for their business. We've gifted our general counsel clients with tumblers of cookies. We've also personally designed Christmas cards, wax-sealed envelopes by hand, and ordered Edible Arrangements® to show that we care.

The Bible instructs us all to act with thanksgiving. This may look different on any given day and in different situations. Nonetheless, acting with thanksgiving, like an elegant and delicious dish, should carry notes of peace and contentment with humble undertones.

WHY IS IT VALUABLE TO BE GRATEFUL?

There's a beautiful story of the power of thanksgiving in Don Gossett's book *There's Dynamite in Praise*:[75]

> A missionary in China was living a defeated life. Everything about him seemed to be touched with sadness. Although he prayed for months for victory over depression and discouragement, no answer came. His life remained the same. He determined to leave his post and go to an interior station where he would pray until

victory was assured. When he reached the new place, he was entertained in the home of a fellow missionary. The first thing he saw on the wall was a motto which read, "Try Thanksgiving."

The words gripped his heart and he thought to himself, "Have I been praying all this time and not praising?" He stopped and began to give thanks, and immediately his heart was uplifted. The missionary went back to his field and experienced tremendous favor, seeing multitudes come to know the Lord. Not only did his perspective change, but so did his life and his work for God.

This missionary's story is proof of how invaluable it is to live in a state of gratitude.

The Benefit of Gratitude for You

The case for gratitude begins in the Word of God, but there are also scientific reasons to maintain an attitude of gratitude. Psychologists Dr. Robert A. Emmons and Dr. Michael McCullough studied gratitude scientifically.[76] In their studies, they compared the demeanor and actions of a group that was instructed to write about what they were grateful for with two other groups. One of the other groups was instructed to write about daily pet peeves, and the third group was instructed to write about things that affected them without an emphasis on whether it was in a negative or a positive way. The research revealed that, after ten weeks, the grateful group was more optimistic, exercised more, and even visited a physician less than the other two groups.

Since the study, gratitude journaling has become a

modern craze. A habit of writing down things we are grateful for and remembering to be grateful has clear emotional, mental, and physical benefits for us all. I can personally attest to the benefits of regularly recording and reflecting on things I am grateful for.

What you're grateful for can be as trivial, grand, or creative as you'd like. I appreciate the wonderful way author Jessica Shaver applies her gratitude:[77]

> I'm a Christian but sometimes I forget to thank God for the things that haven't happened. But not this year. I'm grateful for the accidents I wasn't involved in, the illnesses that never developed, and the times I could have been mugged, but wasn't. I'm thankful my house didn't burn down when I left the iron on for five hours. I'm thankful that when we left the garage door open all night, nothing was taken. Sometimes I forget to thank God for electricity, but this Thanksgiving I will make a point of it. ... I'm glad I have Someone to thank.

The Benefit of Gratitude for the Recipient

Everyone desires appreciation. When we show gratitude to each other, we're esteeming others above ourselves (Philippians 2:3).

According to psychotherapist Dr. John Amodeo, appreciation gives us a sense of value and recognition. It makes us feel liked, gives us purpose, and makes us feel connected to one another.[78] It's no wonder we teach our children at a very early age to say, "Thank you."

But it's not enough to say the words with empty regards—

as we remember I once did with my mother. When expressing gratitude to an employee, a customer, a colleague, a mentor, or a family member, it's important to ensure that the person feels appreciated.

You can achieve this simple goal by expressing *why* you appreciate the individual. You could express your gratitude verbally, but if you want to go a step further, put it in writing. A step beyond that is to give a thoughtful gift. There are innumerable ways to express gratitude. I personally believe that we appreciate receiving gratitude in similar ways to how we enjoy receiving love.

We addressed love languages in the February chapter. (If you haven't read *The Five Love Languages* by Gary Chapman, it's worth the time investment, in my book—yep, pun intended!) As a quick reminder, the five love languages described by Mr. Chapman are: words of affirmation, quality time, acts of service, physical touch, and gift giving. My theory is that if I receive love through physical touch, then I probably appreciate a warm handshake or hug as an expression of gratitude. If quality time is what raises the hair on my arms, then I likely appreciate when representatives go the extra mile to give me special attention and time during my visits to a store. Gratitude can be likened to love and, therefore, can be shown in similar ways.

I personally love expressing gratitude through gifts because gift giving is one of my love languages. I have a history of leaving a sappy thank-you note for my business partner, taking fragrant flowers to my mother to show her my appreciation, and scheduling much-needed massages for my husband to show gratitude for how he cares for his family. However you decide to express gratitude, express it somehow!

EXPLORING THE BENEFITS OF ALTERNATIVE DISPUTE RESOLUTIONS

Another great benefit of expressing gratitude in business is that it may minimize the risk of claims and litigation. Managing expectations, providing great customer service, and offering sincere apologies can help in that area as well. I would offer that genuine humility and gratitude have likely prevented legal conflict for many business owners.

Exuding gratitude may not keep you from all conflicts. In fact, there may be times when legal claims are inevitable. If you find yourself in one of those situations, you may want to consider more peaceful alternatives to litigation, often referred to as Alternative Dispute Resolutions, or ADRs.

Mediation, conciliation, and arbitration are three types of ADRs, which began in the 1970s as an effort to "resolve community-wide civil rights disputes" in addition to addressing the delay and costs associated with the courts.[79] (Doesn't this remind you of Jethro's advice to Moses?)

ADRs are often preferred over the standard lawsuit in court because they are typically less emotional, less time-consuming, and less costly. Most importantly, they work. According to the Department of Justice, voluntary ADR proceedings are resolved over 20 percent more than court-ordered proceedings.[80]

Keep in mind that if you desire to use an ADR option, both parties must agree and submit to its use. Otherwise, one party may pursue litigation instead. For this reason, there are normally clauses included in initial agreements for ADR options that require both parties to comply and, in most cases, would take litigation off the table altogether.

Let's briefly explore the three most common ADRs mentioned: mediation, conciliation, and arbitration.

Mediation

Mediation is a process that allows parties to communicate issues confidentially to a mediator with the intent of coming to an agreement on contended issues. The mediator's job is to listen to the parties' claims, work for the mutual good of both parties, remain neutral, and never force parties to enter an agreement.

Conciliation

Conciliation is similar to mediation, but there are two main differences. First, the parties meet with a conciliator as opposed to a mediator. The conciliator will provide advice to each party with the intent to reconcile the two parties. Second, after having heard the claims and issues, the conciliator is asked to provide a non-binding settlement proposal. Like mediation, there is no requirement for the parties to agree.

Arbitration

Arbitration can be thought of as similar to trials or litigation. Arbitrators hear the case and conduct a hearing, but there are three main differences between arbitrations and trials. Arbitration is private and not open to the public, the arbitrators are experts in the relevant professional field, and arbitrations normally save time and costs. Arbitration awards are enforceable and, at times, require successful parties to go to state court to enforce the award.

Other Christian Options

Some Christians like to use Christian mediation and arbitration. These options are defined the same as above, except the mediator or arbitrator uses Christian principles and resources when assisting the parties to resolve disagreements.

Demand Letters

It is worth noting that we often advise our clients, prior to initiating any claim, to start with a demand in writing. The next step would be for a demand letter to be sent from the law office. Finally, if neither work, submitting to ADR or litigation may become appropriate. If you wish to submit to ADR, you may include this language in your employee handbook for employees or your agreements with your independent contractors, clients, and customers. Remember, you can use ADRs only if the other party agrees.

By now we hope that you fully appreciate the value of CapitalMoms who exude thanksgiving despite the circumstances. Whether to God or to a customer. Whether serving, being served, or engaged in conflict. However you choose to handle a dispute, never neglect thanksgiving.

IT'S DUE SEASON!

In this chapter, we reviewed what the Word says about gratitude and learned the scientifically proven advantages of expressing gratitude. We also talked about some ways other than lawsuits to approach conflict.

Now let's start a gratitude journal! At the very least, consider meditating on what you're grateful for and why at least once a day for the next thirty days.

Here's something you could write in your gratitude journal or recite aloud:

I'm grateful for my children because _____.
(Consider naming each child individually for this exercise.)

I'm grateful for my employee/independent contractor, _____ *(name), because* _____.

I'm grateful for my clients/customers (consider naming them as well) because _____.

Write a thank-you note to a business relation and/or your child(ren) at least once a month for the next six months and *mail it* to the person as a surprise. Even if you do this for your children, they may appreciate seeing their name on an envelope with a stamp. It's a small gesture but, like most small gestures, it could reap great reward.

November Notes

CONCLUSION

The World Needs More CapitalMoms

Wow. If you've made it this far and have implemented the steps in this book, you've been on a journey with us for some time.

Let us begin (or maybe end) by saying, "Thank you." You could have chosen any other book to lead you, but you chose ours. And while we're confident that we have added value to you, we remain humble and grateful.

If you recall, Ebony wrote about the discipline of fasting in the September chapter (feel free to give it a second read!). We now want to challenge you to put that discipline into practice as we wrap up the first round of reading through this book.

Wait. You didn't think it was over, did you?

This guide you hold in your hands is meant to be a forever resource. For example, as you approach your next year of business, you can reevaluate your lists. Things will and should definitely have changed since your first year.

What are your new business goals? How are you going to reach them this time?

Did you think that needing to be reminded to delegate was a one-time thing? No, ma'am.

What about remembering to take a vacation and to love on yourself? We can't preach that enough!

What about kicking fear out the door when it rears its ugly head? Oh, sis, I could live in October.

A great way to assess what may need to be revisited over time is to commit to fasting over these areas at a frequency or in a period that works best for you. For example, seeing as there are twelve chapters and topics, you could choose one per month. Or you could choose the one you struggle with the most. Or you could randomly select one, and regardless of the one you choose, you'll be strengthened, and so will your business.

Let's see what this looks like practically. Below are reminders of each month's focus and a short prayer prompt you can use while fasting:

1. Our preparation (December)—*Lord, help me to organize and prioritize the vision You have placed in my heart.*

2. Our business (January)—*Lord, help me to understand how to articulate my "why" properly and to increase my practical knowledge regarding my "how."*

3. Our customers/clients/employees/families (February)—*Lord, help me to love myself, my clients, my*

business, my family, and all that You have entrusted to me.

4. Our mental health and preparing for the unexpected (March)—*Lord, help me to stay aware of the status of my mental health, to delegate when necessary, and to make sure that I spend time feeding myself emotionally, spiritually, mentally, and physically.*

5. Our cleanliness, protection, and creativity (April)— *Lord, help me to find an ease and balance between organization and creativity.*

6. Our ability to give and serve (May)—*Lord, thank You for the ways You use me to serve others. Help me to see new and exciting ways I can give back that benefit my community and further my mission.*

7. Our faith (June)—*Lord, help me to trust that You are always in control and that my faith will carry me into places unknown with the assurance that You are already there.*

8. Our liberation and confidence (July)—*Lord, thank You for true freedom in your Son, Jesus Christ. Help me to foster freedom in my attitudes, beliefs, community, and workplace.*

9. Our competency (August)—*Lord, allow me to remain teachable.*

10. Our wisdom and planning for the inevitable (September)—*Lord, give me the wisdom and words to have*

what could be uncomfortable conversations with the ones I love in order to protect my legacy.

11. Our courage and boldness (October)—*Lord, thank You that fear has no place in my heart. Help me to recognize when I'm operating out of a fearful place versus a faith-filled one.*

12. Our humility and graciousness (November)—*Lord, thank You for everything You have done, are doing, and will do. Help me to maintain a heart of gratitude.*

Whew!

I know. It was a lot, wasn't it? Ladies, Mompreneurs, CapitalMoms—we want you to know how proud we are of you and all that you have accomplished. This step that you've taken is no small thing. It's life-changing. You are so brave. Thank you again for investing in yourself. Remember: we invest in what we value.

Until next time!

—Ebony and Shai

About the Authors

SHINIA LAMBERT is a mother, an attorney, a managing partner of Jackson Todd & Lambert, PLLC, an author, a speaker, a Bible study teacher, a podcaster, the host of "Rooted: Real People, Real Issues, Real Growth," and a transformative content creator. Shinia currently lives, with all the faith, hope, and love she can muster, in Central Texas with her son Aidan. You can find her on Instagram @Shinia_Lambert and @wearecapitalmoms.

EBONY (JACKSON) TODD was born a military child in Germany and raised around the world. She's a proud Army veteran who served as an attorney before retiring. Now, as a mother of three, wife of an Army officer, award-winning public servant, associate municipal court judge, entrepreneur, radio host, and active member of several organizations, Ebony spends most of her time advising, advocating, refereeing, nursing, hosting, and serving the community. When she finds spare time, Ebony enjoys reading, singing at church, karaoke, writing poetry, and traveling. For more information, follow Ebony on social media @theebonyesquire and visit her website:

www.EbonyTodd.com.

About Renown Publishing

Renown Publishing was founded with one mission in mind: to make your great idea famous.

At Renown Publishing, we don't just publish. We work hard to pair strategy with innovative marketing techniques so that your book launch is the start of something bigger.

Learn more at <u>RenownPublishing.com</u>.

REFERENCES

Notes

- Snowflake icon made by FlexSolution from www.flaticon.com. https://www.flaticon.com/premium-icon/snowflake_2323651? related_id=2323651&origin=search.

- Flower icon made by jocularityart from www.flaticon.com. https://www.flaticon.com/free-icon/plumeria_7091477?term= flower&page=1&position=3&page=1&position=3&related_id=70 91477&origin=search.

- Sun icon made by Eight Black Dots from www.flaticon.com. https://www.flaticon.com/free-icon/sun_312639?related_id=312 639&origin=search.

- Leaf icon made by smashingstocks from www.flaticon.com. https:// www.flaticon.com/premium-icon/aspen_4724181?related_id=472 4181&origin=search.

---

1. U. S. Department of Labor (DOL). "Mothers and Families." https://www.dol.gov/agencies/wb/data/mothers-and-families.

2. Matthews, Gail. "Goals Research Summary." http://www.goalband. co.uk/uploads/1/0/6/5/10653372/gail_matthews_research_summary. pdf.

Dominican University of California. "Study Backs Up Strategies for Achieving Goals." http://www.goalband.co.uk/uploads/1/0/6/5/1065 3372/strategies_for_achieving_goals_gail_matthews_dominican_univer sity_of_california.pdf.

3. Economy, Peter. "Sara Blakely's Most Inspiring Quotes for Success." Inc Magazine. March 20, 2015. https://www.inc.com/peter-economy/sara-blakely-19-inspiring-power-quotes-for-success.html.

4. Henricks, Mark. "Do You Really Need a Business Plan?" Entrepreneur. December 2008. https://www.entrepreneur.com/article/ 198618.

5. Neubert, Mitchell J. "Entrepreneurs Feel Closer to God Than the Rest of Us Do." *Harvard Business School Magazine*. October 2013. https://hbr.org/2013/10/entrepreneurs-feel-closer-to-god-than-the-rest-of-us-do.

6. Lexico, "new." https://www.lexico.com/en/definition/new.

7. Sher, Barbara, and Barbara Smith. *I Could Do Anything If I Only Knew What It Was: How to Discover What You Really Want and How to Get It*. Dell Publishing, 1995.

8. Jansen, Hasse. "94 Mind-Blowing Strategy Execution Stats." Boardview. October 5, 2016. https://boardview.io/blog/strategy-execution-stats/.

9. Jakes, T. D. "Blessed Outside Your Comfort Zone." https://sermons.love/td-jakes/4093-td-jakes-blessed-outside-your-comfort-zone.html.

10. Swope, Renee. "I want to be a woman who overcomes obstacles by tackling them in faith instead of tiptoeing around them in fear." Twitter,

January 29, 2015, 6:00 p.m. https://twitter.com/reneeswope/status/560603340967403520.

11. You can find our videos at: https://www.youtube.com/channel/UCMfkk5Mfw0rU0XdB-JxF_WA/videos.

12. IRS. "Do You Need an EIN?" https://www.irs.gov/businesses/small-businesses-self-employed/do-you-need-an-ein.

13. Based on the New International Version of Romans 4:20–21.

14. Benenate, Becky, and Mother Teresa. *No Greater Love*. New World Library, 2010, p. 69.

15. Gibson, Mel, dir. *The Passion of the Christ*. Icon Productions, 2004.

16. Gibson, Ty. "Frederick's Experiment." Signs of the Times. August 23, 2018. https://signsofthetimes.org.au/2018/08/fredericks-experiment/.

17. Zipkin, Nina. "Study Shows Entrepreneurs Really Do Love Their Businesses Like Their Children." Entrepreneur. April 7, 2017. https://www.entrepreneur.com/article/292568.

18. Halko, M. L., T. Lahti, K. Hytönen, and I. P. Jääskeläinen. "Entrepreneurial and Parental Love—Are They the Same?" *Human Brain Mapping* 38, no. 6 (June 2017): p. 2923–2938. https://doi.org/10.1002/hbm.23562.

19. Alshami, A. M. "Pain: Is It All in the Brain or the Heart?" *Current Pain and Headache Reports* 23, no. 88 (2019). https://doi.org/10.1007/s11916-019-0827-4.

Note: The article cites Dr. J. A. Armour as referring to the "heart brain."

20. Snapp, Cheryl. "To Run a Successful Business, All You Need Is Love." Entrepreneur. September 8, 2019. https://www.entrepreneur.com/article/338787.

21. Farber, Steve. *Love Is Just Damn Good Business: Do What You Love in the Service of People Who Love What You Do.* McGraw-Hill Education, 2019.

22. Chapman, Gary D. *The 5 Love Languages: The Secret to Love That Lasts.* Northfield Publishing, 1992.

23. Rae, Kerwin. "How Kids Spell Love." YouTube video. April 7, 2018. https://www.youtube.com/watch?v=Oy1GlRyHOpA.

24. Burkett, Larry. *Business by the Book: The Complete Guide of Biblical Principles for Business Men and Women.* T. Nelson Publishers, 1990.

25. Robbins, Tony. "Tony Robbins' 20 Best Motivational Quotes." https://www.tonyrobbins.com/tony-robbins-quotes/inspirational-quotes/.

26. Lexico, "madness." https://www.lexico.com/en/definition/madness.

27. Schulte, Brigid, and Stavroula Pabst. "Combating Burnout as a Single Working Parent." Harvard Business Review. June 29, 2021. https://hbr.org/2021/06/combating-burnout-as-a-single-working-parent.

28. Rankin, Lissa. "Are You Addicted to Being Busy?" Psychology Today. April 7, 2014. https://www.psychologytoday.com/us/blog/owning-pink/201404/are-you-addicted-being-busy.

29. Renault, Mary. *The Charioteer.* Pantheon Books, 1983.

30. Kondo, Marie. *The Life-Changing Magic of Tidying Up: The Japanese Art of Decluttering and Organizing.* Clarkson Potter/Ten Speed, 2014.

31. Saxbe, Darby E., and Rena Repetti. "No Place Like Home: Home Tours Correlate with Daily Patterns of Mood and Cortisol." *Personality and Social Psychology Bulletin* 36, no. 1 (Jan. 1, 2010): p. 71–81. https://doi.org/10.1177/0146167209352864.

32. McMains, Stephanie, and Sabine Kastner. "Interactions of Top-Down and Bottom-Up Mechanisms in Human Visual Cortex." *Journal*

of Neuroscience 31, no. 2 (January 12, 2011): p. 587–597. https://doi.org/10.1523/JNEUROSCI.3766-10.2011.

33. Bohn, Henry George. *A Polyglott of Foreign Proverbs, Comprising French, Italian, German, Dutch, Spanish, Portuguese, and Danish, with English Translations, etc.* The British Library, 1857, p. 98.

34. Merriam-Webster Dictionary, "plant." https://www.merriam-webster.com/dictionary/plant.

35. Evans, Tony. *The Tony Evans Bible Commentary.* Holman Bible Publishers, 2019.

36. Daniels, Dharius. *Relational Intelligence.* Zondervan, 2020.

37. Fernando, Jason. "Corporate Social Responsibility (CSR)." Investopedia. March 7, 2022. https://www.investopedia.com/terms/c/corp-social-responsibility.asp.

38. Lego. "In Partnership with WWF." https://www.lego.com/en-us/sustainability/environment/wwf-partnership.

39. World Wildlife Fund. "Lego Group Builds a More Sustainable Future." 2018. https://www.worldwildlife.org/magazine/issues/winter-2018/articles/lego-group-builds-a-more-sustainable-future.

40. Gavin, Matt. "5 Examples of Corporate Social Responsibility," Harvard Business School Online. June 6, 2019. https://online.hbs.edu/blog/post/corporate-social-responsibility-examples.

41. Ethisphere. "Past World's Most Ethical Companies." https://worldsmostethicalcompanies.com/past-honorees/.

42. Lapin, Daniel E., and Rabbi Daniel Lapin. *Thou Shall Prosper: Ten Commandments for Making Money.* Wiley, 2009.

43. IRS. "Exempt Organization Types." https://www.irs.gov/charities-non-profits/exempt-organization-types.

44. Dekker, Ted. *Water Walker: The Full Story*. Worthy, 2014.

45. Kramer Mills, Claire. "Double Jeopardy: COVID-19's Concentrated Health and Wealth Effects in Black Communities." Federal Reserve Bank of New York. 2020. https://www.newyorkfed.org/medialibrary/media/smallbusiness/DoubleJeopardy_COVID19andBlackOwnedBusinesses.

46. Goldstein, Markus, Paula Gonzalez Martinez, Sreelakshmi Papineni, and Joshua Wimpe. "The Global State of Small Business During COVID-19: Gender Inequalities." World Bank. September 8, 2020. https://blogs.worldbank.org/developmenttalk/global-state-small-business-during-covid-19-gender-inequalities.

47. Peale, Norman Vincent. *The Power of Positive Thinking: A Practical Guide to Mastering the Problems of Everyday Living*. Prentice-Hall, 1952.

48. Kane, Libby. "'Shark Tank' Investor: 'Entrepreneurs Are the Only People Who Will Work 80 Hours a Week to Avoid Working 40 Hours a Week.'" Business Insider. July 13, 2016. https://www.businessinsider.com/lori-greiner-shark-tank-entrepreneurs-2016-7.

49. Wolpert, Stuart. "New Mothers' Sleep Loss Linked to Accelerated Aging." University of California, Los Angeles (UCLA). August 5, 2021. https://newsroom.ucla.edu/releases/new-mothers-sleep-loss-linked-to-accelerated-aging.

50. Chamber of Commerce. "Small Business Statistics." https://www.chamberofcommerce.org/small-business-statistics/.

51. Power, Rhett. "A Day of Rest: 12 Scientific Reasons It Works." Inc Magazine. January 1, 2017. https://www.inc.com/rhett-power/a-day-of-rest-12-scientific-reasons-it-works.html.

52. Shirer, Priscilla. *Breathe: Making Room for Sabbath*. Lifeway Christian Resources, 2014.

53. Remen, Rachel Naomi. *Kitchen Table Wisdom: Stories That Heal.* 10th anniversary edition. Penguin Publishing Group, 2006.

54. Gammon, Katharine. "What Is Freedom?" Live Science. June 27, 2012. https://www.livescience.com/21212-what-is-freedom.html.

55. Schwantes, Marcel. "30 Motivational Quotes on Success from Women." Inc.com. November 18, 2016. https://www.inc.com/marcel-schwantes/30-motivational-quotes-from-women-entrepreneurs-that-will-inspire-you-to-succeed.html.

56. Benveniste, Alexis. "The Fortune 500 Now Has a Record Number of Female CEOs: A Whopping 38." CNN Business. August 4, 2020. https://edition.cnn.com/2020/08/04/business/fortune-500-women-ceos/index.html.

57. Beard, Lucas, Jonathan Dunn, Jess Huang, and Alexis Krivkovich. "Shattering the Glass Screen." McKinsey and Company. February 13, 2020. https://www.mckinsey.com/industries/technology-media-and-telecommunications/our-insights/shattering-the-glass-screen.

58. Nelson, Amy. "Women Drive Majority of Consumer Purchasing and It's Time to Meet Their Needs." Inc Magazine. July 17, 2019. https://www.inc.com/amy-nelson/women-drive-majority-of-consumer-purchasing-its-time-to-meet-their-needs.html.

59. D'Eon, Carly. "Millinocket Business Responds to Backlash Over Controversial Juneteenth Sign." News Center Maine. June 22, 2022. https://www.newscentermaine.com/article/news/local/millinocket-business-responds-to-backlash-over-controversial-juneteenth-sign-community-maine/97-f6f105d8-5188-46e3-84a4-cc3beac75b45.

60. Schwartz, David. *Magic of Thinking Big.* Touchstone, 1987.

61. Lexico, "knowledge." https://www.lexico.com/en/definition/knowledge.

62. Brown, Brené. *Daring Greatly: How the Courage to Be Vulnerable Transforms the Way We Live, Love, Parent, and Lead.* Penguin Publishing Group, 2012, p. 186–187.

63. *Quote Junkie: Motivational: An Incredible Collection of Motivational Quotes Designed for True Quote Enthusiasts.* CreateSpace Independent Publishing Platform, 2008.

64. Statista. "Fear of Death in the United States in 2019." October 2019. https://www.statista.com/statistics/959347/fear-of-death-in-the-us/.

65. Grossman, Cathy Lynn. "Billy Graham's Quotes About Heaven." USA Today. February 21, 2018. https://usatoday.com/story/news/nation/2018/02/21/billy-grahams-most-notable-quotes/858852001/.

66. Caring.com. "2021 Wills and Estate Planning Study." https://www.caring.com/caregivers/estate-planning/wills-survey/.

67. Donoghue, Emma. *Room.* Oberon Books, 2017.

68. Lexico, "fear." https://www.lexico.com/en/definition/fear.

69. Shirer, Priscilla. *Fervent: A Woman's Battle Plan for Serious, Specific, and Strategic Prayer.* B&H Publishing Group, 2016, p. 105.

70. The BAW$E Conference. February 25–27, 2022.

71. Hayes, Deborah. "What Are Mergers and Acquisitions (M&A)?" December 31, 2021. Investopedia. https://www.investopedia.com/terms/m/mergersandacquisitions.asp.

72. Sweeney, Deborah. "Dissolutions, Withdrawals, and Reinstatements: How Do These Terms Impact Small Businesses?" SCORE Association, November 2021. https://www.score.org/blog/dissolutions-withdrawals-and-reinstatements-how-do-these-terms-impact-small-businesses.

73. Angelou, Maya. 2018. "I've learned that people will forget what you said, people will forget what you did, but people will never forget how

you made them feel." Twitter, September 2, 2018, 12:59 p.m. https://twitter.com/drmayaangelou/status/1036327789488734208.

74. Moore, Beth. *Living Free: Learning to Pray God's Word*. Lifeway Church Resources, 2015.

75. Gossett, Don. *There's Dynamite in Praise*. Whitaker House, 1974.

76. Emmons, Robert A., and Michael McCullough. "Counting Blessings Versus Burdens: An Experimental Investigation of Gratitude and Subjective Well-Being in Daily Life." *Journal of Personality and Social Psychology*. https://greatergood.berkeley.edu/pdfs/GratitudePDFs/6Emmons-BlessingsBurdens.pdf.

Emmons, Robert A., and Michael McCullough. *The Psychology of Gratitude*. Oxford University Press, 2004.

77. Brown, Edmund Sackey. *Principles for Rising Up in Life: Your Pathway to Achieving Your Dreams*. Xlibris UK, 2010.

78. Amodeo, John. "Why We Like Being Appreciated." Psychology Today. April 23, 2016. https://www.psychologytoday.com/us/blog/intimacy-path-toward-spirituality/201604/why-we-being-appreciated.

79. United States Agency for International Development (USAID). "Alternative Dispute Resolution Guide." https://www.usaid.gov/sites/default/files/documents/1868/200sbe.pdf.

80. United States Department of Justice. "Alternative Dispute Resolution at the Department of Justice." 2017. https://www.justice.gov/archives/olp/alternative-dispute-resolution-department-justice.

Made in the USA
Coppell, TX
02 December 2022

87589757R00174